HOW I BECAME A MAN

Alexander N. Krylov

HOW I BECAME
A MAN

*A Life with Communists, Atheists,
and Other Nice People*

Translated by
Michael J. Miller

IGNATIUS PRESS   SAN FRANCISCO

Translated from the second German edition of
Wie ich zum Mann wurde:
Ein Leben mit Kommunisten, Atheisten
und anderen netten Menschen
© 2021 by fe-Medienverlag GmbH, Kisslegg, Germany

Cover art:
The Crucifixion (1497)
Kirillo-Belozersky Monastery, Vologda Oblast, Russia
© HIP/Art Resource, New York

Cover design by Roxanne Mei Lum

Contents

Prologue

It happened a few years ago now. I was living at the time in Moscow near the famous Novodevichy (New Maidens') Monastery. One day, as I opened the door to my house, I could scarcely believe my eyes. The street was full of merchants, soldiers, officers, farmers, women, and children from the nineteenth century. They wore funny old clothes, walked past my house, and spoke with each other about their normal, everyday problems—money, shopping, or family conflicts. Wherever I looked, there was not one single modern man far and wide. "Something is not right here", I thought, and walked for a while with them. Only at the end of the street did I learn that on the frozen monastery pond they were about to film a fair from the year 1895 for a historical blockbuster. And so thousands of costumed extras had to walk from their buses along our street to the location for the scene. In the crowd of people from the nineteenth century, I almost could have doubted my sanity. One simple lesson from this experience: In a crowd you can easily become confused.

So it was, too, for some people in the Soviet Union. I was born there and grew up in that Soviet system. What is offensive to us today or seems comical or even dumb appeared self-evident to us then. It was self-evident that we should honor Lenin, praise Communism, or wear a red neckerchief. It was also self-evident to laugh, to hope, to seek, and to believe. Normal humanity and insanity were often so close together that they could scarcely be distinguished.

For more than twenty years now, I have been living in Germany and have been asked again and again, first by my students, colleagues, friends, and acquaintances and now by members of my parish, also, to tell them something about life in the Soviet Union. Even if hundreds of books on the subject are written and numerous documentaries are filmed, private experiences are still more exciting. Along with my analytical lectures, I began to tell true stories from my childhood, thus lending some flavor to the dry accounts. It took a good friend of mine, Christian Rickens, whom I also value highly as a journalist, more than ten years to motivate me to write down and publish my stories and anecdotes about life in the Soviet Union. And here we are.

I did not contrive the credible and the incredible events in this book, but just wrote them down as I lived and experienced them at the time. All these curious stories and sad incidents, strokes of luck and surprising discoveries, were part of my growing up. This is not my biography, nor is it the chronological summary of my childhood. These tales of a youngster who wanted to grow up to be a man are typical of many other human beings who lived in the Soviet Union and tried to come to understand their reality; they are tales about people who in different ways were striving to be good, to bring joy to each other, and to learn the meaning of life.

So I invite you to begin a journey with me into a land that no longer exists and is even somewhat surreal in order to become acquainted with many people there, among them Communists and atheists, too, through the experiences of an altogether ordinary child in an altogether ordinary private environment.

In the Beginning Was Love

Love at first sight, regardless of how romantic it may be, can be accompanied by many surprises. When my father got to know my mother better, he had to make serious decisions and offer loving sacrifices. For my mother's name then was Ida Graf and her nationality was German, which in Russia twenty years after the war was not an unqualified advantage. Besides that, my mother's family had suffered under repressions and therefore was not allowed to move to Moscow with my father. Quite by chance, my mother landed together with my grandmother in a little working-class city in the European part of the Southern Ural region. There, during a business trip, my father became acquainted with my mother and decided to move away from Moscow to the provinces for the love of his life.

The chief town of the district, with around 40,000 inhabitants, was similar to many other Soviet cities. It was distinguished, however, by its good infrastructure, because of its location along the river running between the picturesque Ural Mountains and the distance of almost 1,240 miles from Moscow. Through this city, through its many inhabitants, along with their customs and practices, we will get to know life in the Soviet Union in the 1970s and 1980s from the inside and often look at life in the outside world, too.

We notice first that this is a very green city, whose streets

sink into a sea of green. With its many parks, bridges, boule-
vards, and fountains, it leaves one with a contented feeling about life. Here we find seven schools, a trade school,
a boarding school, and many kindergartens. Beside Lenin
Square stands the Cultural Palace, built in the classical style,
and farther on there is the House of Culture, three cine-
mas, four libraries, the House of Young Engineers, and the
House of the Pioneers. And then three hospitals, three poly-
clinics, a sports palace with a large swimming pool, a soccer
stadium, and a skating rink. In a woodland park, a novelty
was installed—Fitness Street—a parcours with many pieces
of exercise equipment.

Almost everything was available to the townspeople at
no cost. And yet we experience this city as a working-class
city. A relatively small, flat area between the mountains was
the site of an important steel mill, a light bulb factory, a
chemical plant, two construction companies, and a furniture factory, along with a dairy plant and an industrial bak-
ery. The rhythm of the city was defined by a long-drawn-
out siren that every day announced the beginning of a new
shift at 8:00 A.M., 4:00 P.M., and midnight. Among the urban
elite were Party officials, teachers, doctors, creative types,
and several families that had come to the Ural region from
Moscow and Leningrad during the wartime deportations.
Despite the magnificent landscapes, hard work made the people rough and hard. Coexistence between individual human
beings could be described at first sight as rather coarse and
not exactly friendly. Our family had no relatives in the city
and no social set, and even after several decades, we still felt
like strangers in these surroundings. The nicest memories in
this city were provided, not by the beautiful natural scenery
or the cultural institutions, but rather by people.

For my parents, starting a new family was associated not

only with difficulties but also with joys and anecdotes. As a professional from the capital, my father not only got a good job but also a three-room flat (which in those days was considered large) in the first high-rise apartment complex of the city. At that time, my aunt lived in another corner of the countryside and only seldom could visit my mother. Shortly after the wedding, she decided to surprise her sister by showing up as a guest unannounced. She showered and began to wait for her sister. When my father rang the doorbell after work, a complete stranger, a woman in a bathrobe with a towel wrapped around her head, opened the door for him. "Excuse me, my mistake", said my father, and went away.

Back on the street, he looked around: all the apartment buildings, constructed according to the same plan, looked the same. He had not written down the address, and they did not have a telephone then, either. Now at that moment he no longer knew where he should go: in the place that he thought was home there was apparently a different family; the city and the people were unfamiliar and strange. To his joy and relief, he saw my mother coming. One year later, I too came into the world, and our family assumed its complete form.

Apartment houses can look alike; cities can live according to a similar rhythm; families can have the same problems. Yet every individual life is unique; it has not only its own ups and downs, but also unique and often surprising twists. Everyone can discover for himself that God's ways are unfathomable.

Lifelong Kindergarten

We children liked to tell each other about our wishes and dreams. Fireman, pilot, soldier, and even veterinarian, ice cream salesman, film projectionist, or baker—these were the occupations most often wished for in our group. But I wanted one thing above all—to be grown up. Grown-ups do not have to eat this thick gruel every morning; they are not forced to lie in bed for three hours after the midday meal. Grown-ups can go wherever they want and do whatever they want. They can even make decisions themselves and be free. In spite of a good kindergarten teacher who loved us, and in spite of an educational program with a lot of variety and all the efforts of Soviet pedagogy, I was always happy at the end of the day to be back with my parents again.

The best scientists in the country worked to make socialist education attractive and long-lasting. Little children could already look forward to it in the crib, because at the age of nine weeks they were handed over to state education. From the state's perspective, this had many advantages: they could avoid bourgeois formation and family ties, lay the foundations for collectivist behavior, and bring the mothers back into the labor market as soon as possible. Then there was also the naïve thought of training parents by way of their children. If the children acquired Communist values, ideally they would thus influence the grown-ups also to live by these values.

In the progressive kindergartens, a so-called five-day stay was offered. The parents dropped the child off early Monday morning and picked him up again on Friday evening. No wonder many fathers were not quite sure which one of the children they were supposed to take home with them on Friday. I was brought to the kindergarten each day at eight o'clock in the morning and picked up again at five in the afternoon. Pragmatically speaking, the kindergarten had everything necessary to give the children a happy childhood. We could play, sing, and dance, we went for walks, visited movie houses, and celebrated all sorts of holidays. The only thing that was not provided for us was our own individuality. For everything served a higher purpose—to develop in us the feeling of We. I sensed this almost daily during naptime. Since I never liked the midday nap, our kindergarten teacher, who was actually very kind, constantly had to punish me. It was no fun standing alone in the corner with my face to the wall when all the other children were allowed to play. So one day I announced my decision to live an independent life from now on.

No sooner said than done. I talked a girl into escaping with me from the kindergarten. We had decided to start our own pre-school in a little garden with wild apple trees that I once saw in center city. The two of us even managed to leave the kindergarten secretly and to set out on the way. This dream was shattered when we had almost arrived at the goal. For then my accomplice noticed that she had forgotten her doll and absolutely wanted to go back. I was not happy about this unreliability, but I could not let her walk through the streets alone. To our great surprise, this adventurous excursion into the great wide world went completely unnoticed and, hence, unpunished, too. I had to wait another few years to become a grown-up and to have an independent life. At that time I did not yet know that grown-ups, too, have their problems with being grown up. For everyone, life in an ideological system was like being in a kindergarten: the state provides for the citizens, keeps them busy, and educates them. Where independent people who think for themselves are not needed, one is actually never allowed to become a grown-up—in other words, life-long kindergarten.

My First Sermon

Back then, I never saw a church or a priest, and yet, as a five-year-old child, I gave my first sermon. At least my kindergarten teacher thought so. Once when I discovered that all the other children knew nothing about God and had not even heard anything about Him, I called together almost the whole group of children and informed them who lives in heaven and all the things that He does for us. We were outside on the kindergarten playground and were looking at the blue sky, in which only a few clouds and an airplane vapor trail could be seen. As I was making this announcement, which did not conform to the established educational guidelines, I was caught by my kindergarten teacher. She was a loyal Soviet citizen and assured me that there is no God. She told us that our first cosmonaut, Yuri Gagarin, had already been in space and had seen no God there. Therefore, she said, only stupid, uneducated people believe in God; they were wasting their time and even hampered our progress. We all loved this kindergarten teacher very much. Her words were so convincing to me that I could hardly wait to bring this fascinating news home.

"Grandma, you don't have to pray any more. Yuri Gagarin was in heaven and saw no God up there!" That was the first thing I said when I came home. Unfortunately, I can no longer remember what answer I got, but the discrepancy between the experiences of cosmonauts and our own experiences of God has been of little concern to me since then.

A correct religious education was not possible in those days. My grandmother and my mother, with their previous political experiences, did not dare to give me a religious upbringing or to teach me anything specifically for that purpose. God's presence in everyday life, though, was self-evident for our family. In Grandma's room hung a picture painted by my uncle that showed the merciful Jesus with two angels on a mountain. My grandmother walking through our apartment with her rosary in hand also belonged to our regular daily routine. No one taught me prayers or religious attitudes, but in our family God's existence was not at all in question. He was simply always there with us. My former kindergarten teacher belongs today to the Russian Orthodox Church and not only is a staunch believer but also proclaims the Christian faith. We said no more to each another about the theological experiences of the cosmonaut Yuri Gagarin.

Caught as a Spy

In the 1970s, Soviet television broadcast a twelve-part series, "Seventeen Moments in Spring", about a Russian spy in the Reich Main Security Office. Everyone was talking about the film, and it showed how disciplined and organized the Germans were in the Third Reich. The suspenseful presentation had established certain stereotypes and prejudices so firmly that I could sense it even as a little kid. There was no hiding the fact that half of my family was German. My grandmother was very loquacious but spoke only broken Russian and made no secret of her family's heritage. With my Russian surname, I was at first not suspected of being a foreign agent, until a puddle detector changed everything.

Whenever it rained, a big puddle formed in the courtyard of our high-rise apartment building. One day, the neighbor boys were having fun playing in this puddle. They would run and jump into the middle of the puddle, so that the water splashed on all sides. They were enjoying this tremendously. I had just come out of the building and looked at what was going on in the courtyard. One lady on the second floor who was watching the whole game commented very loudly: "Look, now: this boy over there does not get dirty but stands aside so neat and proper. You can tell right away that he is a German." And she also repeated a saying that can be translated approximately as: "A bear is still a bear when you ship him elsewhere." Another woman immediately added, "People like that will surely leave our Soviet land at the first opportunity." Leaving the Soviet land was then considered serious betrayal. At that moment, I wanted with all my might to jump into the puddle to prove that I was not a foreigner and not a traitor. But the other boys had already walked away from the puddle, so that it no longer made sense to play alone in the puddle. Then I went home, almost in tears, to ask a serious question: "Mama, are we different?" It did not take much to feel like a stranger in one's own surroundings. The Soviet land has long since been history, but unfortunately stereotypes and prejudices exist in every country and at every time. Even a puddle can be enough to get you caught by a neighbor as a foreigner.

A Russian Soul

When my mother applied for admission to university around ten years before I was born, she traveled to a large industrial town and began looking for a job. She went from one business to another and inquired whether they were looking for a secretary-typist. At the front desk of one business, two security guards were so involved in a discussion that my mother could not interrupt them at all, and she simply went in. Since she found no one on the premises to talk to, she went back. This time they asked her for her visitor's pass. "I don't have one", my mother replied. The security guards could not believe that she had been able to get past them so easily. Meanwhile, my mother had no idea that she had ended up in a military facility involved in the production of atomic weapons. Now she was detained and questioned. When the security staff saw her I.D. card, they suddenly turned pale: Ida Graf, German. On a Soviet identity card, the nationality was always noted. It was scandalous that fifteen years after the war, a German woman could simply walk without permission into a top-secret military facility. The security guards feared for their jobs, and that ultimately rescued my mother. She had to certify in writing that she would tell no one about this incident, and then she was allowed to go.

The life of Soviet citizens was full of secrets. The government kept secrets not only from other governments but also from its own citizens. The citizens kept secrets not only from the government but also from each other. In our city, there was no street map and no detailed topographical map, either—everything was a secret. Actually, even the children knew about all the secrets. The grown-ups told stories about what secret production was taking place in what factory. But psst! You are not supposed to tell anyone. So we children grew up amid strict secrets. But Russia's biggest secret was and remains, not its military might, but rather the Russian soul. My grandmother once wished that I might have a German head and a Russian heart. Of course, I was curious, then, about what that was supposed to mean and began to explore the hearts and souls of the people around us.

Especially on winter evenings, when it got cold and dark outside and there was nothing interesting on television, neighbors would come over. Without a special invitation or appointment, you could knock on the door and thus pay a neighborly visit. Alexandra Vasilyevna—an old *babushka* on the fifth floor—often came to visit my grandmother. In the neighborhood, she was addressed simply by her patronymic [father's name], Vasilyevna. Since she had been born before the October Revolution, she could relate things about village life in the days of the tsars. Often she even brought a spinning wheel with her, and while she spun or knit socks together with my grandmother, she began to tell stories or sometimes to sing Russian folk songs. For me, the stories from her life were like fairy tales from which I could learn something about Russian folk customs and even about the Russian soul.

When Vasilyevna was still very young, she and other girls of the same age tried to find out their future companions through fortune-telling. The best time for that—she said—is Christmas Eve, the time just before Christ comes into the world. She was sure that candles, water, mirrors, and even fur-lined boots could help find out the name of the bridegroom, the number of children, and the sentiments of the in-laws. After her wedding, she stopped playing with fortune-telling, because such games, she said, are very dangerous. If you bring evil spirits into the house, it is very difficult to get rid of them again. She had plenty of examples of that.

Vasilyevna also told about how, after the Revolution, the Communists closed the village church and burned up the icons and the prayer books. Out of fear, Vasilyevna, too, took her little icon off the wall, wrapped it in a cloth, and stored it in the back corner of the silo. Several days later, she sensed that someone was present in her house. Once at night she saw a woman dressed in white sitting in the corner where the icon had hung. Vasilyevna asked the woman what she wanted and received the answer: "I would just like to know why you hid me in the silo and why you no longer wish me to stay with you." The next morning, Vasilyevna brought her icon back into the room and never again was parted from it. When she died, this icon was even laid into the grave with her.

I could tell that the Russian soul is a mystical soul. But that does not yet fully describe this soul. People try to become acquainted with it through the works of Pushkin, Dostoyevsky, or Tolstoy. The famous Russian author Ivan Turgenev wrote that a real Russian has the heart of a child. Many say that the Russian soul is a melancholy, unpredictable, compassionate soul in search of meaning. When you try to explore it, you understand that it conceals a secret. Just like the top-secret facility in this story. No strategy can help you get into it. Rather, you get into it by accident, and then you are surprised at all there is to discover inside.

The Blue Spots

In the evening, when the whole family had already gone to bed and the light was turned off, my grandmother would begin her secret mission. She had a little bottle of holy water in her hand and walked through the whole apartment with it, to bless us all and to place our night of rest under God's protection. Even my father, who was not particularly enthusiastic about the Catholic faith, made as if he did not notice this at all. I, on the other hand, often stayed awake a little longer in order to get the blessing.

Incidentally, the holy water was produced domestically. There was neither a priest nor a church where we lived at that time. So where did we get the holy water? On all Church holidays, my grandmother placed a little cloth mat on the table, brought her old colorful holy cards out of her prayer book, and put them on the sewing machine. In this way, she arranged her own altar. On Easter and on the day of the Baptism of the Lord, a bowl of water always stood on this altar, too. When a priest somewhere in the world blesses water, then he blesses our water, too—my grandmother was firmly convinced of it. The water from that day was decanted into little bottles and remained fresh throughout the year. We likewise were convinced that somewhere in the world a priest was praying for us, too, and giving us a blessing every Sunday. Today when I occasionally celebrate Holy Mass alone, I pray for all those people who cannot go to church, and at the conclusion, I give them a blessing, too. Maybe even today there is still someone who, like my grandmother, is waiting for a blessing for herself or for her bowl of holy water.

Despite or thanks to all the successes of scientific atheism, many people in our area were superstitious. When a black cat or a woman with an empty bucket crossed your path, when a person forgot something and quickly went back home for it, or when a glass broke—nothing good could be expected. A neighbor's child broke an expensive crystal bowl. His mother praised him nevertheless, because at that moment he had not forgotten to say over the shards of glass, "May it bring good luck."

Now a neighbor lady learned that my grandmother blessed our family every night with holy water. She asked her for a little bottle of holy water and decided from now on to protect her loved ones from evil spirits. Not long afterward, she mixed up the little bottles in the dark and, instead of holy water, took blue ink. The next morning the family could not explain at first why on the bedclothes, on the furniture, and on the walls there were numerous ink spots. Only when the blue-faced perpetrator wished everyone a good morning did it become clear where the spots had come from. For that night she had sprinkled herself, too, and rubbed ink evenly over her face. Superstition is therefore not only useless; it can also leave dark spots.

My Moscow

There are little cities and big ones; they may be old or young, beautiful or less beautiful. There are also cities that have their own soul. Even as a little child, I was able to discover the soul of Moscow and to learn to love it. For this city not only made an impression on my life but also gave it salt and pepper.

During the summer vacation, when children are normally brought from Moscow into the provinces, I was driven from the provinces to Moscow. We had many relatives there, on both my mother's and my father's side. I spent most of the time with Aunt Maria and two of my cousins. This time was in sharp contrast to our life in the Ural region. There were impressive edifices, great broad streets, and countless people from all sorts of countries and cultures. You could get the best ice cream in the country here and the best chocolate. What a joy it was for me when I was once photographed with the world-famous clown Oleg Popow in one of the best children's programs in the country, *Budilnik* [alarm clock]. I was enchanted by the many churches with fantastic onion domes and also by the subway stations that looked like cathedrals. In the center of the city, you could still find the house where our ancestors had lived before the October Revolution. The gigantic city taught me to go beyond my own limits and also to reflect on diversity and freedom.

But our visit to the Tretyakov Gallery was like an excursion into another dimension. Countless large paintings showed me an unknown reality and gave wings to my imagination. I can remember clearly the time I first discovered the Icon of the Holy Trinity by Andrei Rublev. It is difficult to say exactly what it was about this old and, at first glance, somber depiction of three angels that spoke to me as a boy, but I remained standing in front of the icon and even prayed secretly. My intention was that the grown-ups, too, would find their way to God sometime and that all people would be allowed to pray. In the time between vacations, I liked to read stories about Moscow and graphically imagined historical events.

I took it for granted that I had two native cities, even though this involved certain difficulties. The Muscovites liked to make fun of the provincials, of their behavior, their clothing, and their narrow-mindedness. In the Ural region, in contrast, nobody was interested in what I had seen or experienced in Moscow. "Don't put on airs", our elementary-school teacher said to me once when I dared to add to her story about Moscow. She herself, like almost all my friends then and many adults, had never been in Moscow and could scarcely imagine life in the capital. Moscow, therefore, brought me not only enthusiasm but also difficulties and doubts. Nevertheless, it was very enriching to be at home both in a working-class city and in a great metropolis. You could learn a lot from each one of the many encounters and from each experience.

Among my first memories of Moscow is a scene at the fountain. I was still a little whippersnapper when my grandmother told me that neat clothing and shined shoes say a lot about a man. Now when I saw a man with rumpled, misshapen trousers and shoes with worn-out soles, I felt obliged to enlighten him. I went up to him and asked if he did not know that good people would wear clean trousers and clean shoes. Then I spat at his feet. Of course, this situation was embarrassing for my parents, and they began to apologize for me. The stranger kept walking, and I noticed that my well-intentioned words had missed the mark. A few minutes later, this man stood in front of me again. He smiled at me and gave me ice cream on a stick, which I loved so much. So Moscow taught me for the first time to correct my perception of the world. A man is much more than his appearance. Even in the capital.

The Wake

The whole block was probably awakened by that scream. It was Aunt Lyuda—our neighbor from the third floor. Grown-up friends of the family were often addressed by us children as Aunt or Uncle. Aunt Lyuda had always had a panicky fear of corpses, and she said that she would never forget that night. Early in the morning, she already was sitting in our apartment, and, although at that time she had nothing to do with Christianity, she asked my grandmother to say a prayer. Then she started to tell her story from the beginning.

When she was still a child, she participated in a wake in her village. It was already evening, and the villagers sat in front of a coffin lying in state. After a rather long interval of silence, someone began telling weird stories about the spirits of the dead. It got creepier and creepier, and suddenly something happened that is actually normal and yet does not occur that often. The remaining gases that were still present in the corpse suddenly poured out through the mouth, so that the dead man "exhaled" deeply and loudly. Grown-ups and children—everyone jumped up and ran away, not only through the doors but also through the windows. Ever since then, this Aunt Lyuda had had a panicky fear of dead people.

The mystery of death was quite evident in our life, despite materialism and atheism. In Moscow and in other major cities, burials were performed somewhat differently, but in our region it was not difficult to see how Communist rituals mingled with religious customs. The burial took place according to the Orthodox understanding, on the third day after the person's death. Anything else was a rare exception. Until the burial, the open coffin always lay in state in the family's residence, so that not only relatives and friends but also neighbors and colleagues could bid farewell to the dead person. Such a direct encounter with death caused even Communists and atheists to reflect on whether death ends everything or whether there might be something beyond death after all. Despite fears of being labeled reactionary Christians, grown-ups on such occasions recounted in a whisper many inexplicable incidents in their acquaintance with death.

On the day of the burial, all the relatives and anyone interested met outside on the street. A day before that, a monument welded out of metal with the name and the photograph of the deceased person had been set up in front of the entrance. That way everyone could know that a burial was being prepared in this house. I do not know the reason why, but it always started at 2:00 in the afternoon. The open coffin was first carried outside and then through the streets. All the people and all the automobiles stopped. Old *babushkas* were sure of it: If anyone overtook and passed the coffin with the deceased, he himself would soon end up in the next world. We children were afraid of the dead, and yet we often ran behind funeral processions and, out of curiosity, tried to catch a glimpse of the corpse. For the deceased embodied a mystery—something that was not spoken about publicly, which was far beyond all our human ideas.

The funeral procession was led by a truck decorated in black, which carried the monument. From this truck they threw fresh fir cones onto the street. Over these fir cones the coffin lid was carried first and then the coffin. If the deceased was not too old or was especially notable, a brass band marched directly behind the coffin. Then the family and relatives followed, and everyone else who wanted to go along.

After the interment at the cemetery, the funeral parties in our city ended up at the reception in a café that specialized in this, which oddly enough was called Café "Youth". The customs that had become fused with superstition determined what drinks and foods had to be served in any case. For simple people, it was important to place a little glass of vodka for the deceased at the grave or on the table. Some were even afraid that the deceased himself would appear to his loved ones in a dream and complain about the poorly organized burial. A woman waiting in line at the grocery store related how several times in a dream she saw her departed husband weeping and begging. She drove 75 miles to the nearest church, requested that a Mass be offered for him, and organized the memorial meal. After that, the departed left her in peace. Indeed, it was the custom, besides the meal after the burial, to invite people to memorial meals on the ninth and the fortieth day after the death. Even the local Communist officials secretly followed all these customs. The only difference between Communists and Christians could be seen at the monument: in one case, the star was depicted on it, and in the other case—the cross.

Now I come back to the heartrending scream and to our neighbor, Aunt Lyuda. She was summoned during the night by the militia as a witness, because her neighbor from the apartment across the hall had killed himself. The corpse was lying in the corridor, blocking the entrance. In order to go anywhere, Aunt Lyuda had to step over the body. She turned away from the dead man's face and began to step over him. The militiaman noticed that Aunt Lyuda was unsure of herself and tried to support her with both hands —precisely from the side where the corpse's hands were. It is really a miracle that the scream that followed did not wake the dead man, too. Forever afterward, Aunt Lyuda suspected that dead people were pursuing her. Since there were no prayer books then, she took a notebook and from that day on started to copy by hand various prayers for all sorts of occasions. Wagging tongues said that that was the only good thing that the dead man had left as an inheritance.

Alternative Currency

Actually, I was a brave boy. I could stay in a dark room alone without any fear, and I was not even afraid of dentists, injections, or black cats. What I really feared as a child was a drunk. Often next to the grocery stores, in the municipal parks and even on public benches, you could see drunken men around a bottle of vodka. For many people in the Soviet Union, planning leisure time without alcohol was unimaginable. Vodka was everywhere—in private life, on the job, and even on television. Many people tried to produce vodka themselves, and they died of alcohol poisoning. Numerous rituals and traditions developed around alcohol. In no case were you allowed to imbibe alcohol without a toast, to put the full glass of vodka down after the toast, or to refuse to drink to someone's health. As far as vodka is concerned, I took up a clear position while still of kindergarten age.

We lived in a five-story high-rise apartment complex that consisted of four staircases and seventy apartments in all. A neighboring family from apartment 5 was celebrating a wedding. Such festivities started on Friday and lasted until Sunday. Many customs, games, and silly assignments were part of the fun. I was five years old when I went home after playing and met a rather tipsy wedding party in front of the door to the building. A drunken man blocked the door and let in only those who were willing to drink a shot glass of vodka to the health of the newlyweds. When he saw me, he came up on all fours and said, "Well, young man, soon we will celebrate a wedding for you, too." Before then, I had never seen a drunk at such close quarters, and I noticed that his behavior was not normal at all. I felt unsafe and began to scream so loud that a crowd of people gathered around me. When I had calmed down somewhat, I turned to them and announced: "Do what you want; I am not playing along. And I will never drink your vodka and never celebrate a wedding with you!"

But there were also plenty of people and families for whom alcohol was not very important. And yet most of them had at home a small supply of vodka. In our house, too, about a dozen bottles of vodka were in the cupboard for an emergency. Back then, vodka was the best insurance. When something broke at home, it was very difficult to find a handyman. For 3.5 ounces of vodka, neighbors helped with little repairs; for a complicated job, you had to offer the whole bottle. In situations where there were no government services and you could make no headway with money, you paid in liquid currency.

Permanently Sealed

You can be baptized only once in your life—everyone knows that, at least those who have had some dealings with the Church. Unintentionally, I was not only baptized twice but also received First Holy Communion twice and was confirmed twice. On the day of my first Baptism, I was just seven days old and cannot remember this very important event at all. Maybe that was because I was concerned too much about my physical well-being and thought too little about the Church. Since the nearest Catholic priest could be found at a distance of around 1,250 miles, my grandmother baptized me herself. In many Catholic families, this was the only possible way of baptizing children at that time. Not only the Catholic but the Orthodox Church, too, was not to be found in our region. I first set foot in a Russian Orthodox church when I was six years old; in a Roman Catholic church, not until I was twenty.

Three months before I started school, my mother drove with me to a health resort in Western Ukraine. One day, we discovered there an Orthodox church building and went in. It was a whole different world inside, another dimension that we had never seen before and never experienced before. It was relatively dark, but not frightening. Candles were burning everywhere. Many people looked at me from the ceiling and from the walls. Only later did I learn that they were Jesus and the saints. Their faces looked quite different from the faces that I usually saw on Soviet posters—they radiated love and joy. Their bodies were almost transparent and floated. Incense and the singing rounded off this impression. "Let's stay here forever; we can bring our prayers here", I whispered to my mother. Would my first impressions of the Church have been like that if instead of icons I had seen modern church art or pictures by Sieger Köder [a German priest-painter, 1925–2015]? Even externals can play a role in some circumstances.

Throughout our vacation, we went to church daily. For me, the Divine Liturgies in those days were even more fascinating than the children's carousel or the zoo. As time went on, there were two women who spoke about me with the local "pope" [Orthodox priest]. The pope was very unsure about "baptism by grandmother" and suggested baptizing me again. The two women strangers became my godparents. Although they were very devout, they secretly warned us to be careful in dealing with the pope. No one knew who he actually was. . . . In those days, some popes worked for the KGB. I can remember my second Baptism very well. Just like my second First Communion and the second Confirmation. We just did not know that First Communion and Confirmation are administered at the same time as Baptism in the Eastern Churches, and that is why I received both sacraments in the Catholic Church, too, as an adult. From the theological perspective, it made no sense to receive these sacraments twice. For me, they were not only beautiful experiences but something that gives my life a firm grounding and permanently seals my union with God.

Healthy Diet

Nowadays there are many people who watch what they eat and try to convince others about the value of a healthy diet. The basic rules of a healthy diet, according to current magazines and talk shows, are simple: not much meat, not much fat, vegetables and fruit only in season, and predominantly local produce, and it is best to do without exotic fruits. When I look at life in the Soviet Union from this perspective, I discover how much the Soviet government cared about people's health. Indeed, all the rules mentioned here were taken for granted on an everyday albeit involuntary basis.

While in Moscow there was still a greater selection of foods, the situation in the provinces and especially in the Ural region was quite different. Everyone tried personally to make sure of his own survival. Almost all families had a little allotment garden, where not only apple trees, cherry trees, and currant bushes but also potatoes and many other vegetables were planted. These gardens played a major role in the health of Soviet citizens and made sure that from May to September they got enough exercise, had a hobby, and thus consumed less alcohol.

At harvest time, marmalade was cooked in every household, pickles and tomatoes were canned, and sauerkraut was produced. Many of our neighbors and acquaintances prepared big supplies every year in a hundred or so three-quart canning jars. Another challenge was storing it all. My family kept vegetables and homemade preserves in a garage that we had built specially for storage purposes.

Only rarely could meat be found in the grocery stores. A well-known joke describes a man who comes into the grocery store. "What? You have no fish today?" The storeclerk answers, "No, there's no fish across the street. Here there's only no meat." In the 1980s, food stamps were introduced. In order to spare the prestige of the Soviet Union and avoid criticism from the West on account of food shortages, these stamps were called "order certificates". According to this concept, the groceries were "pre-ordered" by the consumer and then picked up at the store. Everyone received two of these order certificates a month, each for 11 ounces of meat or sausage, and another certificate for 7 ounces of butter. Still you could often buy chickens without "pre-ordering". Thanks to the poor work of the chemical industry, they were raised with no additives and usually looked as though they had walked by themselves from the chicken factory to the grocery store.

Meat and many other groceries were lean as a matter of principle and usually dry, too. All this helped us, on the one hand, not to overeat and, on the other hand, not to waste food, either. One item always of excellent quality was chocolate from Moscow. The chocolate factory of the German confectioner Theodor Ferdinand von Einem was renamed "Red October" after the Revolution and continued to produce candies in the German tradition. But this chocolate, too, was rarely for sale in the grocery stores.

In any case, our diet was good for the government, too, since the life expectancy of sixty-five years for men and seventy-four years for women meant less of a financial burden on the pension system. When the government takes over full responsibility for the health of its citizens, everyone has to cooperate, even though the individuals do not really want to know exactly what in fact is good for them. And so it was compulsory for us to learn what has become fashionable today: to live in harmony with nature and to appreciate how precious groceries are.

Lenin Sees Everything

What a wonderful man Vladimir Lenin is. We learned that
already in kindergarten. In school, right from first grade on,
hardly a day went by without talk about Lenin. His portrait
in a gold frame was hung in every classroom over the blackboard, so that he could always look at us with his wise and
somewhat sly glance. Even on the playground in the municipal park, there was a statue depicting the little Volodya (so
Lenin was nicknamed) sitting on an armchair and watching
the children.

All pupils were qualified to wear Lenin's picture on their
school uniform. Even in first grade, seven-year-old children
were initiated as October Children. You got a red star, too,
with the picture of little Lenin in the middle. At the age of
ten, you were accepted into the Young Pioneers, who were
obliged to wear a red neckerchief and a Pioneer star every
day. Depicted on this star were the head of Lenin and three
tongues of fire. I shared with no one my impression that
this star depicted the head of Lenin burning in hell. At the
age of fourteen, the students could prove their maturity by
membership in the Communist Youth League—*Komsomol*.
Lenin's head was depicted this time on a red flag. Thus,
Lenin's image, like a pectoral cross, was always supposed to
be worn close to the heart.

Soviet authors wrote many stories about Lenin in order

to help us children be able to grow up into truly good human beings. As a child, for example, Volodya broke a carafe belonging to his aunt and could not admit it at first. For two months, he was quiet and pensive, and he told everything that had happened only when his mother found the child in bed crying. He was a very honest man and, except for this one case, never lied. Lenin's example was supposed to support us children, too, as we learned, since Lenin not only was endowed with a prodigious intellect but also could plan his workday well. He disciplined himself to do various sports exercises and gymnastics while he was a student. Moreover, Lenin was not only a shrewd thinker, he was of course good at bicycling and an excellent swimmer. We learned that he was good-hearted from the story when he went hunting but did not shoot at the handsome fox or when he bought a toy for a working-class child. We learned how he outsmarted a policeman, how he donated to poor children a fish that had been given to him, or how later on, as head of the government, he used to wait in line at the barbershop like everyone else.

After stories like that, no one doubted that Lenin was the greatest moral authority and the most humane of all men. Every child should strive to become like him. Even though Lenin had died, he still remained eternally present to the Soviet people and was particularly close to children. When our elementary-school teacher had to leave the classroom once during instruction, she pointed to Lenin and said, "I will be away for a moment, but Lenin sees everything!"

The Other Ecumenism

Officially, most people in the Soviet Union belonged to no religion, or they were staunch atheists. Unofficially, it was known who was a Christian, who was a Muslim, and who was a Jew. We never heard technical terms like "interreligious dialogue" or "ecumenism", but we lived them. There were no ecumenical projects and initiatives; there were no corresponding programs and efforts—there was, though, an unexpressed wish: to support one another in faith. Whenever someone died, everyone who knew prayers and could pray would meet at the home of the bereaved. No special appointments were made; everyone met with an obvious respect.

I learned from my grandmother what an interreligious dialogue really is. She was a staunch Catholic, and yet she saw an ally in every human being who was seeking God. With her simple diplomacy, she managed to come to an agreement with the Orthodox Christians and Muslims in our neighborhood. Religious holidays were mutually respected: on these days no laundry and no hard work was done. The first time I saw Muslims praying on television, I was still an elementary-school student. I found their many bows amusing and began to imitate them, laughing. To this day, I have not forgotten my grandmother's comment: "Don't make fun of them! Just think, these men are turning to God." So

42

I understood that communication with God can happen in various languages and forms.

For us, it was a special joy when we had our Lutheran acquaintances over to visit. In our area, there were only three German families—two Lutheran and ours, which was Catholic. Since we had the larger apartment, we all met at our place on important holidays for one prayer service. On those days, much German was spoken and German hymns were sung. Often the conversations between our guests and my grandmother developed into heated theological discussions. The two sides disagreed then, but on the next possible occasion, everyone met at our place again. After all, common prayer was much more important than any disagreement.

I myself could not recognize any differences between Catholics and Protestants, except probably for one. When one of our Lutheran acquaintances was visiting us for the first time, she introduced herself to me as Aunt Agatha. During the midday meal, I started to tell a story. Suddenly Aunt Agatha pounded the table with her fist and cried, "While eating I am deaf and dumb!" I was rather startled at the time, but it was explained to me that Lutherans are particularly strict and austere. Since in our house, we used to discuss a lot of things at meals, at first I found this rule not good at all. Only because Aunt Agatha was otherwise very communicative did I accept her peculiarity. For a while, I even thought that the main difference between Catholics and Protestants consisted precisely in this, that we speak at meals and they remain silent and think only about God. For further insights, you need more maturity first.

How I Became a Man

During that night, my father, who for months now had been in the hospital, visited me. I asked him to stay with me, but unfortunately he had to go. When he closed the door behind him, I woke up. It was dark, and I was afraid. That is one of the few dreams that I can remember. At five o'clock that afternoon, the mailman brought a telegram from Moscow: My father had died the previous night, on March 3, at 3:00. I ran from one room into the other and sobbed. For logistical reasons, I was not taken along to Moscow for the burial. In spite of my uncle's higher-ranking position and a certain distance that he kept from the Church, a church funeral took place.

After the burial, I understood that now I was not only a child but also the one man in the family and that, with my seven and a half years, I already had to take on a responsibility for my mother and my grandmother. I told this to other children from my neighborhood. Edik, who was four years older than I, thought that becoming a man is a particular moment. You would sense it in your whole body and would never forget it. At the time, he did not mention that, for that, you need a woman, too.

A few months later, I decided to take my manly duties in the household seriously. I began to tighten up the loose electrical outlets in the apartment. As I was carrying out these repairs with the screwdriver, I saw fireworks. I flew

44

back a few meters, and my hand turned black. When I came to again, I brushed the rust off my hand and went to see Edik: "It was all just like you said. Today I became a man."

During an attempt to paint the bathroom, I dribbled so much paint on my head that they had to shave off all my hair. It was embarrassing, but I could not stay sad for long. Life went on. My mother, who was raising me alone, received forty rubles a month from the government for my education, and I could also drink one glass of milk per day for free in the school cafeteria.

During that time, I also learned to pray, and the thought never occurred to me to blame God for our situation. On the contrary, I pitied God, since He had to care for us even more in these circumstances. All told, He did a super job of managing everything, despite the whole adventure and the risks that I ran. I was able to help and could always find new, exciting chores for myself. Becoming a man is not a particular event but, rather, a process; you understand this only when you have grown up.

The Green Patrol

I first contributed to the cause of protecting the environment when I was still in elementary school. For five kopeks
I received a record of my contribution and also a membership card in the Nature Conservation Society, and until
graduation I regularly paid my dues. Our teacher had told
us how important it is that everyone should not only be a
conservationist personally but also actively take a stance and
to point out environmental problems to others. In school,
we regularly discussed relevant newspaper reports, and once
we even saw a children's film about young conservationists.
In this film, schoolchildren had formed a "Green Patrol"
and on their own initiative showed grown-ups how we can
protect our environment.

The Communist Party (there was no other one then)
was very supportive of children's activities in nature conservancy. It is good when children and youths do not think
about fundamental political and economic questions but,
rather, busy themselves with plants and butterflies. So the
"Green Patrol" was praised throughout the country. It was
obvious that we children, too, wanted to do something for
the future of our planet. Together with Alyosha—a boy
from my neighborhood—I then decided to start our own
"Green Patrol". After my grandmother sewed two green
armbands for us nine-year-old boys, we set off without de-
lay to patrol through our city and heroically to stop everyone who was ruining the environment. After a good hour,

we were already tired but still had found nothing suitable for our heroic deed. Then my conservationist comrade noticed a dog lying on a flower bed. "The dog is destroying the flowers, which are important for nature and especially for the bees. We must arrest the dog and hand him over to the militia", Alyosha said. We found a clothesline and took the dog along. Several minutes later, an old man on the street said that it was his dog and asked us to give it back to him. "The dog is arrested and will be handed over to the militia", Alyosha said. The old man was so charmed by our zeal for nature conservancy that he offered to pay us a fine for the dog. We received a valuable fifty kopeks in return for the dog. I suggested bringing this money to the militia, but Alyosha was of the opinion that we should do something good with the money. He was able to convince me to spend the money on a movie. At the end of the day, we were happy—nature conservancy is a win-win: for the flowers, for the bees, and even for the conservationists themselves.

What the Climate Determines

"For a child, there is nothing better than to catch a cold in the winter", a girl from our school once told me. Sick people in the Soviet Union not only got humane attention but, in addition, the opportunity to stay at a health resort. Several times I witnessed grown-ups trying to outdo each other, arguing about which one of them had more illnesses. A child who had a cold was not only allowed to stay at home but also received round-the-clock care. Usually a cold was treated with many natural medicines such as herbal tea or linden-flower honey. Considered particularly effective against fever were the homemade raspberry preserves that were saved especially for the sick. A child with a cold received many visits from friends and acquaintants, who then brought along fruit (which was rare then) or sweets.

Even better than a cold for us children were extreme freezing temperatures. When the thermometer showed less than -22° F, we had off from school. At that time, it was not possible to regulate the heat at home yourself. People were supposed to know that the government cares for them. Central heating was so called also because it was managed centrally. The colder it was outside, the warmer it was inside. Winter decorated the windows with enchanting ice flowers—not only on the outside. During an extremely cold spell, a layer of ice formed on the inside of the glass, too. During a snowstorm or a blizzard, it was especially fascinating to melt the ice with one finger and to watch the natural spectacle from this homemade peephole. You could see how the individual passersby in thick fur coats fought with the snow and the wind as they walked home. Inside, in contrast, it was very warm and cozy. You had time to read something about the exciting adventures somewhere on the other side of the world or to watch fairy tales or animated cartoons. Once I was, nevertheless, bored at home during such weather and decided to walk to a nearby grocery store to get fresh bread. Stories were often told about one or another person losing fingers, ears, or a nose because of frostbite. You do not joke with extreme freezing weather.

When it was not so cold during the winter vacation, we liked to spend time in the courtyard or on the street: we built snow forts or conquered the mountains of snow that had already been built; we sledded down hills of snow that we ourselves had piled up; we had snowball fights or played ice hockey without skates. We went skiing every week during sports instruction at school. Thanks to my winter gear, such as a fleece coat, a muskrat *shapka* [hat], and very warm felt-lined boots, I often stayed outdoors for hours, despite the cold. There was so much snow that once in the dark I sank so deep into it—up to my head—that I could no longer extricate myself. Fortunately, a passerby heard me shouting and got me out of that pile of snow. It was not bad, though—every one of us boys could tell stories like that. After playing, we often went together to the house of someone in our group. It was cozy and warm there, a kind word awaited us, and there was also hot tea with pancakes and jam. In the winter, warmth is especially necessary and especially noticeable. Even if someone claims a monopoly on interpersonal climate, the warmth of the heart cannot be managed like district heating. We children were able to learn this even despite the cold political climate.

Always Ready

We liked to celebrate birthdays. They were among the few festive occasions that were simply human. For the government and the Party, it made no difference whether and how someone celebrated his birthday. There was, however, one birthday that no Soviet person forgot. On April 22, the whole country celebrated the birthday of Vladimir Lenin. On this occasion, in every school and in every business, there was a festive meeting at which certificates of honor were awarded to the best students or workers. On this particular birthday, I was admitted in third grade to the Young Pioneers together with all my classmates.

"I am so proud of you, because it is a great honor to be called a Pioneer", our teacher, Valentina Vasilyevna, told us. "Only someone who is a Young Pioneer can grow up to be a good human being. Since you have now grown so big, you can help as Young Pioneers to improve people's lives and contribute to the welfare of the whole world." Whenever someone shouted, "Be ready to fight for the cause of the Communist Party!" we had to reply "Always ready." The teacher said, "That means that you should be ready to do good."

The prospect of becoming a good human being and helping others appealed to me. Despite the marching and many rituals that accompanied it, I was very glad to be a Pioneer. I was overjoyed when I was elected by our class to the school's Pioneer council.

I waited impatiently for the first assembly of the council in order to receive a task at last and to begin my activity for the welfare of mankind. The meeting was conducted by the state-appointed Supreme Pioneer Leader. At the beginning, she said that our first duty was to take minutes of the meeting. What it meant to take minutes was difficult for me as a ten-year-old to understand. "You must write down the most important ideas in a notebook specially designed for this purpose", the stressed Supreme Pioneer Leader explained. I did not dare to ask a follow-up question. In the next three meetings, we talked only about making announcements and writing reports for all sorts of panels. "Something is not right here", I thought, and spoke up with the question: When would we finally start to do good? Again it was difficult to grasp why this simple question made our Supreme Pioneer Leader angry. She demanded my notebook to inspect it and became even angrier. Since I had found no important ideas in the previous reports, I began to write down my own observations in the minutes. So the reader could find in this notebook a record, with the exact time indicated, of the facts that Olga smelled like cooking oil, that there were holes in Marina's uniform and that the Supreme Pioneer Leader had yellow teeth. I could not understand why my zeal to do good and my true interest in my fellow human beings were rewarded with expulsion from the Pioneer council. Despite an initial unsuccessful attempt to do good as a Young Pioneer, I was always ready for all sorts of campaigns for the welfare of mankind and even for the welfare of the whole planet. I eagerly collected waste paper and recycled metal, planted trees, and looked after the elementary-school children. Something I was never again ready to do, though: take minutes.

The Something Principle

As schoolchildren, we constantly had to participate in various activities, sports events, group projects, and initiatives. This participation was obviously voluntary. In those cases where the will of the children was nevertheless too weak, the activist or the teacher of our class always helped out: "Why were you not there with all the other children in order to help our homeland?" The stupidest thing would have been to answer this question in an argumentative way, because each argument was followed by a negative judgment. Forgetting, oversleeping, or missing the opportunity was not as bad as reflecting on the substance of the activities. Someone who is not an activist is simply an egotist; he does not love his homeland and does not want to contribute anything toward our future and the future of the whole planet. Personally, I found many of our children's campaigns interesting. You could in fact help other people and even learn something for later life.

The book by Arkadi Gaidar, *Timur and His Team*, was familiar to all Soviet children. It was about fourteen-year-old Timur Garayev, who together with other children secretly provided aid in their neighborhood for relatives of soldiers. Thus a Timur-Aid campaign started not only in the U.S.S.R. but also in many socialist countries. We children rang at the apartment doors and at the houses of war veterans, their wives, and other elderly people in order to help them with their housework. Even though for some people our help was burdensome rather than supportive, they nevertheless let us into their apartments. Such an encounter not only stayed in my memory but even influenced my later professional life and my leadership style, which is connected with it.

Once we children helped an old *babushka* tidy up her room. There I found a single tablet on the floor, which had probably fallen under the bed and lain there for a while in the dust. I picked it up and asked, "What should I do with this tablet?" The *babushka* immediately snatched it from my hand and swallowed it. "Why are you taking this medicine, when you do not know what it is good for?" I asked thoughtfully. "Oh, it will be good for something", the *babushka* replied. I decided then to note this story well. Not only in the Soviet Union but everywhere in the world, in contemporary politics, in business, and also in the renewal of the Church, decisions are often made according to the principle of this *babushka*: The main thing is to take action—it will be good for something.

Whistling Investigator

My mother worked as the head economist and director of a planning department, which in the framework of the planned economy was the third-most-important position in the municipal construction firm. She had to work many hours overtime; I found that not so bad, because from five o'clock on, I was allowed to go to her office and play with her arithmometer [a mechanical calculator]. While still in elementary school, I became acquainted with many of her coworkers and the security guards and had the privilege of running around everywhere in the depot, playing with the watchdogs and even activating the button for the entrance gate. Mechanics, truck drivers, or carpenters all found time for me and showed me their machines and all sorts of tools. Workplace safety was limited at that time to posted warnings, and so I tried to work with all sorts of machines by myself. Most of the guards were already of retirement age and liked to tell me something about their lives, about the war, and even about their family problems over tea in the guard booth. As time went on, I knew what building materials were stored where, where the keys to the workrooms were hidden, and even where some construction workers drank their beer after closing time.

Once an officer from the department of criminal investigation came to our house. During the previous night, the carpenter shop had been broken into and robbed, and so he had a few questions and asked me to help him with the investigation. This would have made any boy especially proud, because everyone wanted to be a detective someday. No doubt I understood the conversation with the investigator as an official delegation, and so I prepared for my mission. The first suspects were the workers in the carpentry shop itself. Stealing from one's employer was commonplace. Since according to the Soviet philosophy everything belonged to the people, the people also felt justified in arbitrarily making use of the people's property. Therefore I did not find this suspicion credible, because it made no sense for employees to break into the carpentry shop. Everyone could take whatever he wanted home with him through the open entrance gate. The guards thought that still showing up at work at all for their low wages was good enough, and they had no interest in making a fuss.

Now I received the assignment of finding the stolen goods and tracking down an unknown criminal band. At five o'clock, I armed myself with a plastic revolver, took a whistle, a magnifying glass, and a flashlight and started to conduct my own investigations in the depot. I got into the carpentry shop through a back door and took up a lookout position. I did not have to wait long at all until a man appeared with two wooden beams. Then I jumped out of my hiding place and began blowing the whistle with all my might. Startled by the whistling, the thief dropped the beams on his feet, and I heard loud cursing. However, it was not a thief, but rather the carpenter Andrei Pupei, whom I had not recognized in the half-light. He was not at all angry with me but, instead, praised my courage and sent me home. A few days later, the real thieves were tracked down. The stolen goods were lying the whole time right next to the guard booth. So my only criminal case to date shows that what you are looking for can sometimes be found right in front of your nose.

Magic Tricks Revealed

In early April, our elementary-school teacher asked us what we were going to celebrate in the coming days. My classmate Vitya, who sat beside me on the same bench, immediately raised his hand. One would have expected him to speak about Cosmonautics Day, since every child was supposed to know that on April 12, 1961, our Soviet citizen Yuri Gagarin was the first man in outer space. Instead, Vitya started to talk about Easter and solemnly announced: "Next Sunday we will celebrate the Russian folk festival *Pascha*."

Our teacher, Valentina Vasilyevna, was short, plump, with a round red face and a potato nose. When she heard Vitya's answer, she became much redder in the face and began to scream. I had never see such rage before and wanted to hide under the desk. She said that it is impossible that anyone in the twentieth century should still be talking about Easter. Only stupid, uneducated people could say such a thing, because Soviet students did not believe in God but, rather, in the power of the human intellect and in scientific progress. For that whole class period, Valentina Vasilyevna could not calm down. Every one of us learned from this example the lifelong lesson, that there are topics that one must never mention in public. Only later did I understand why our teacher, whom we really liked, reacted so violently. She screamed out of fear. For the school administration or the school inspectors might have thought that she taught us topics like

Easter. For the time being, anything having to do with God
and faith became taboo for us.

In fourth and fifth grade, in addition to school instruction, we had atheism classes. Once older students came to
our room and showed us magic tricks, which could be seen
in the circus, too. With such magic tricks, they said, priests
stage "divine miracles" and deceive naïve people. Through
the efforts of the young atheists, we could see this decep-
tion with our own eyes, so as to be able to explain it to
ourselves. We also learned that priests are criminals and that
the religion of the capitalists serves to oppress the working
class.

From the government's perspective, it was unnecessary
to deal in greater depth with questions of faith. The ori-
gin of life and similar questions, they said, had been explained definitively by the established dogmas of scientific
materialism. Where the world is going and what mankind
expects could be learned from the writings of Karl Marx
and Friedrich Engels. There was no need to seek for the
meaning of life, either, because the only way to find this
meaning was to build up Communism—sometimes even
by sacrificing your life. It was not possible at all to question
these postulates publicly. In a trusted circle, however, people often discussed inexplicable scientific phenomena and,
in the case of illnesses, prayed secretly, too. Anyone who
could not discover the meaning of life in Communist writings tried to find it in alcohol or somewhere else. It took
years for gullible society to recognize that its attempts to interpret the meaning and goal of life by prefabricated world
views and Party dogmas were only ideological magic tricks.

Olympic Signs

The only summer in which we had to postpone our trip to Moscow was the summer of 1980. That summer, the Olympic Games took place in Moscow. Everything possible was done to prevent unnecessary contacts between Soviet people and foreigners and also to supervise the city better. Alcoholics, homeless persons, criminals, and many suspicious types were forcibly resettled and were not allowed to live closer than 63 miles away from Moscow. Identification papers were checked at the train stations of the capital, ostensibly for the welfare of the citizens, and anyone who did not have a permanent residence in Moscow had to turn back. During the Olympic Games, therefore, I was not in Moscow, and yet I had a clear memory of these games. We were all proud of our country and of our Soviet sports. In summer camp, we cheered for the athletes at the same time as the guests at the Olympics, sang along with the popular tune "Evenings in Moscow", and let our tears of joy flow at the same time as the Olympic Bear.

After all the foreigners had traveled home, I was allowed to try Pepsi and Fanta in Moscow for the first time in my life. It was probably a unique event in history, but these two soft drinks of the stiffest competitors [i.e., the United States and West Germany] were produced in the same beverage factory in Moscow. At first I thought that Pepsi-Cola must be an acquired taste, because it reminded me of some medicines. On the other hand, I was enthusiastic about ice-cold Fanta. We were familiar with juices and natural lemonade only, but no artificially produced beverages. Fanta, then, was much more orange-y than oranges themselves. "It would be cool to breed a new variety of orange that would taste like Fanta." Thanks to the Olympics, we tried salami, canned ham, and instant soups for the first time. At that time, all departments of life revolved, therefore, around the Olympics.

The Soviet government did everything possible to get children excited about sports. In my hometown, there was a sports palace, a sports school for children and youths, a stadium, and many sports clubs. You could use practically everything for free. As a prelude to the Olympic Games, morning gymnastics were introduced in the schools. At the beginning of the first period, we were obliged to do morning exercises in the gymnasium. Later, these were relocated to the classrooms. Our sports teacher gave us instructions over the school radio, and we tried, between the rows of desks, to imitate some moves. A duty is rarely fun.

For us boys, it was fun to visit our sports clubs after school and to play soccer in the evening on the lawn of the apartment complex. After completing a checklist of achievements in various kinds of sports, you could submit your GTO qualifications and in return receive a bronze, silver, or gold medal. GTO was an acronym that meant "Ready for Work and Defense". Some of our fellow students had to train a lot for these medals. Others received the same awards later on with no effort whatsoever, because the school had to fill its quota of excellent athletes.

I had a similar experience with my first bicycle, which I got during the Olympic summer of 1980. The Olympics logo was affixed to this bicycle, to the envy of all the boys. "That is a sign of the special Olympic quality; it will hold it all together", the salesman told us then. He definitely knew what he was talking about. A half year later, when this logo fell off, my bicycle broke down, too. Awards, documentation, and honorary titles played a major role not only in public life but also in sports and had a magical effect on many people.

Once on the train, I had the opportunity to become acquainted with a genuine master sportsman of the Soviet Union. That was the official honorary title for the best athletes in the country. Before that, I had seen such highly respected personalities only on the TV news. The sleeping car consisted of nine compartments, for four passengers each. The master sportsman of the Soviet Union sat in our compartment. I joyfully told the conductress about this unusual passenger. She was able to make use of this information when in another compartment two drunks started a brawl. The mere threat by the conductress that she would go and get a master sportsman from a nearby compartment was enough to break it up. When such a strong man is riding along in the train, there are no worries about keeping order. Afterward, the conductress asked us: "Whom should I thank?" I had overheard the quarrel and already knew what she meant. "Him!" I said, pointing to a short, slender, bald man who was sitting across from me. "Him? Are you a master sportsman of the Soviet Union?" She could scarcely believe it. "For what sport?" "Yes, I am", the man assured her. "I am the master sportsman in chess."

Christmas Eve

On the Soviet calendar, there were many different holidays, but no Christmas. Some people knew, though, that the Orthodox Church celebrates the birth of Christ on January 7. This played no role in the life of an ordinary family. The fir trees [*Tannenbäume*], the festive meals with the whole family, and the gifts were customary on New Year's Eve. Most people had no idea whatsoever about the Catholic celebration of Christmas Eve on December 24.

For us, Advent was not associated with any special traditions; it was just a dark and cold season. I do not know how my mother got it, but on Christmas Eve we always had an evergreen tree. When a fir tree comes from a frosty forest into a warm apartment, it begins to fill the whole room with a special, Christmas-y freshness. Now we could decorate the living room, too, with lights and streamers. At that time, there was no crèche; instead, in a special place we set up old holy cards with pictures of the Nativity. Grandma kept these in her prayer books throughout the year, and they did not appear again until the Holy Night.

When everything was prepared, we waited for nightfall. The only church that we could visit was a mawkish village church depicted on an old holy card. Grandma read prayers in German and Latin; then we sang German Christmas carols. It was a special joy to tune in to broadcasts from a Western radio station. Sometimes we managed to hear *Stille*

Nacht, "Silent Night", on Deutsche Welle or Vatican Radio. It was like a voice from heaven, a proof that we were not alone in our faith, but were united with an invisible world-wide Church. Only after midnight did we sit down at the table. For Christmas, the best that could be obtained then was prepared. Almost always there was aspic [jellied meat], egg salad, warm *Fleischkuchen* [meat pie], canned vegetables, and homemade varieties of fruit preserves. Often there was red caviar, too, or even ham from the West.

On Christmas Eve, I was allowed to stay up late. It was particularly fascinating for me to look through the frozen window at the sky and to try to find the Christmas star. The street lights were no longer shining, and light could be seen in no other window. In our home, though, candles were burning and the string of lights on the Christmas tree was blinking. The next morning I had to go to school and unfortunately could not share the joy of this Christmas Eve with any of my classmates. I was convinced, though, that on this day, all children, even the atheists, were under God's protection. It was somehow implicitly clear that God does not abandon human beings as long as a light is burning in at least one window on Christmas Eve and at least one person is waiting for the Christ Child.

The One-Eared Rabbit

Every year in November, the parents of the students in our class formed a holiday committee. The only item on the agenda was to obtain New Year's presents for us. Every child paid one ruble. The parents tried to find something tasty in the stores for this money and even traveled to other cities and regions to make purchases there. Then they counted every single piece of candy and divided them up into little bags. Many adults still remember today what could be found in a gift bag like that: a dark red apple, an orange, two tangerines, and six to eight delicious chocolate pralines, and a lot of simple bonbons. But the effort that went into it shows how highly the New Year's celebration was prized in our country.

Actually, New Year's Day was the only ideology-free holiday on the Soviet calendar. After religious holidays were forbidden in the Soviet Union, the Communists noticed that a replacement for Christmas was needed. And so many traditions sprang up around the New Year's holiday. We could not imagine at all that these characteristic Russian traditions were a Soviet invention. On this family holiday, even the grown-ups felt as though they were in a fairy tale, in which it was possible to combine simple human joy with mystical hope for new happiness.

The most beautiful event in the year for children was the *Jolka* holiday. Translated, *jolka* means fir tree. In every school and in every business, a decorated evergreen tree was set up in the middle of a large common room. Children came to this celebration in costumes and took part in games and skits. The wicked powers tried to prevent the arrival of Jack Frost and his granddaughter, the Snow Maiden. Good prevailed, however, and every year Jack Frost managed once again to bring along the gift bags that had been prepared by the parents. Everyone present sang New Year's songs, held hands, formed a circle, and danced around the fir tree. The most important *Jolka* celebration in the country took place in the Senate Palace of the Moscow Kremlin. For the children, there was a magnificent stage show and selected sweets in a plastic gift box shaped like the Kremlin, but meanwhile the grown-ups had to stay outside.

One Jolka Day in kindergarten, my grandmother sewed an astrologer costume for me: a long, dark cape with gold stars stitched onto it. When I came to the kindergarten, I saw that all the girls were wearing snowflake outfits made out of gauze. All the boys except me were rabbits. That was the simplest costume for a boy: a white shirt, white leotards, black shorts with a little round cotton tail and two white cardboard ears fastened to a headband. Now suddenly I thought that my elegant costume was dumb, and I wanted to be like all the other kids. When I started to cry, the teacher gave in and put together a rabbit outfit for me. There was just one problem. She had enough cardboard for only one upright ear, and we had to make the second out of regular paper and let it droop. One year later, though, I came to appreciate my astrologer costume. I wore it to my first Jolka celebration at school and was even honored by Jack Frost with an extra present.

On December 31, the approaching holiday was already in the air, and everywhere—on the street, in school, in the workplaces—you could sense a special anticipated joy. The holiday meal was prepared like a little wedding, for most people were convinced: "The new year will be as good as the celebration that welcomes it in." In the late afternoon, three hours were reserved for the television comedy "Irony of Fate" that was repeated every year. The real celebration began around two hours before midnight. Certain foods like the Russian egg salad "Olivier" (named after a French chef), aspic, sprat [a saltwater fish], and "herring in a fur coat", and "Soviet champagne" were indispensable at the festive table. At around ten minutes before midnight, the speech by the government leader was broadcast on television and the bells of the Spasskaya clock tower in Moscow rang in the New Year. When I became a teenager, I was allowed to walk through the streets with my friends after midnight. Everywhere you could hear music and season's greetings. On the main square of the city, which was decorated with fir trees and ice sculptures, a festive entertainment program was performed.

Most people today who think back to the time in the Soviet Union like to remember the New Year's celebration. For people, it was much more than a tradition and much more than consumption. Not only the children, but the grownups, too, felt that the last night of the year was magical. It showed that people can find their happiness even without Christmas. Happiness in which no one had to become the astrologer [and watch for the appearance of the first star on Christmas Eve], but some were content even with the role of the one-eared rabbit. And yet the New Year's celebration was also a sign of yearning. A yearning for what is good and noble, for love, attention, security, and ultimately also for God.

The Career of a Heartbreaker

When I opened the door, an unfamiliar man suddenly stood in the entrance hall of our apartment. "Hey, who all lives here?" the stranger asked. I was at home alone. Something was not right, but as a nine-year-old child, I did not know at that moment how I should react. Many neighbors had only one key to their apartment and left it under the doormat while they were away. So somebody could find keys under many doormats and get into their apartments with no problem. That is why even I had no misgivings about opening the door to someone. In this situation, with a stranger in the apartment, I was fortunate that an officer's cap was hanging on the wardrobe. "Do officers live with you?" the man asked. "Yes", I answered without hesitating. I meant myself. When our balcony neighbor, Uncle Yura, gave me this cap as a gift, he said that now I, too, was an officer in the Soviet Army. I especially liked to wear this cap when playing hide and seek with the boys. The stranger did not want to confront an officer and immediately went on his way. Several days later, a peephole was installed in our apartment door.

There was great respect for the military. The anniversary of the founding of the Red Army on February 23 was declared the holiday of the Soviet Army and was celebrated throughout the country as men's day. Men were honored as protectors of the fatherland and of their families and received gifts on this day from women. In school on

February 23, there was a competition for the best slow march, and as a reward each class received a big sheet cake with hot apple marmalade. The girls in our class wrote us greeting cards, and every boy felt like a real man. Being a man, according to a statement by our teacher, always had something to do with calm, composure, and politeness toward a woman. In her opinion, the best men were the officers. They were genuine knights: athletic, intelligent, and they could even break the hearts of young women. I did not understand the last remark at first. But one day an opportunity arose to learn more about heartbreak.

Edik, who was four years older than I, decided as a little kid to go into the armed services. He had even set out to make a real officer out of me. For my part, I tried to pass on what I learned to his brother, who in turn was three years younger than I. "The most important things for an officer are fearlessness, steadfastness, and endurance", Edik used to say. As training in these qualities, he shut me into his parents' wardrobe and made me promise that I would not leave the wardrobe unless he ordered it. Since it was certainly boring for him to sit beside the wardrobe, he went outside shortly afterward. There he met one of the boys in our group and forgot all about me.

In the wardrobe, it was dark and narrow. For some time I was even afraid. Then I thought of God: If He is everywhere, then He is certainly also in this wardrobe. From then on, it was no longer unbearable for me to wait, because we two were sitting in the wardrobe: the Lord God and I. As time went on, waiting became more and more difficult. I could have opened the door from inside and gone away. But I could not do that, because I had given Edik my word. Now, finally, I heard footsteps. But it was not Edik. I tried to be even quieter than before. Someone lay down on the bed, and it became quiet again. The time seemed like an eternity to me.

Now, finally, I heard the footsteps go away, and I got into a better position in the wardrobe. At that moment, the wardrobe door opened and in front of me stood Edik's mother. She was home for the midday break to take a short siesta. If someone had been able to take a photo at that moment, he would have preserved for all time a scene full of drama, facial expression, and emotions. "What are you doing here?" she asked me in a very small voice. "I am guarding your apartment", I answered carefully. "What a scare you gave me! It breaks my heart", she added in the same wispy voice.

And so on Soviet Army Day, I could not only display loyalty and bravery but also infer what heartbreak is. It had something to do with hiding in the bedroom. Today, I cannot say precisely why as a nine-year-old I had already ended my career as an officer. It may be that it had something to do with heartbreak.

Wilted Carnations Day

In many businesses at that time, there was a Lenin Room, or so-called "Red Nooks", where assemblies and Party activities took place. Sometimes I came along for such meetings, which were open to adults only. For instance, a yearly assembly on International Women's Day on March 8, at which the women were honored.

Already in elementary school, we learned that Women's Day developed from an initiative by Clara Zetkin at the Second International Socialist Women's Conference. We did not learn, though, that, along with equal opportunities for women, they were also striving for their emancipation from family and children. The historical documents record many recommendations for abolishing the family and leaving the education of children completely to the government. Among the new initiatives were the introduction of women's quotas and the legalization of abortion and the battle against the Church. They hoped to achieve the development of a new reality by changing the language. The grammatical gender of some words was made feminine, while other words, in turn, were made masculine. Women did, in fact, acquire many rights in the Soviet Union, but as time went on, the feminist campaign was abolished and replaced by reverence for the working woman.

The assembly in honor of working women that I was allowed to observe at my mother's place of business con-

sisted of many solemn speeches for the occasion. At the conclusion, each woman received a handshake from the Party
chairman, who also gave her a red carnation. Again and
again, I was able to witness the same scene on March 8: In
the first rows sat the women, exhausted after a hard day's
work. Surely they wanted to go home to their families and
appeared rather unmoved. Just like the long-since-wilted carnations that each one held in her hand. Therefore, in my
recollection, the joy of the celebration is associated with
exhausted women and wilted carnations.

As time went on, these celebrations became less and less
ideological, but also more bourgeois and mawkish. I sus-
pect that even the Party leadership approved this development, because the women were no longer fighting for their
rights but let themselves be praised and honored. Now the
focus was no longer on rights but on gifts and consumption. In those days, it was also customary for the men to
take over the housework on March 8 and to cook for their
families. Since at that time housekeeping and cooking were
understood to be exclusively women's work, the men usually had not learned to do either. In our circle of acquaintances, anecdotes were often told about how the women's
great March 8 expectations led to many disappointments,
from burnt, inedible food to clumsy cleaning.

We children, too, celebrated March 8. In kindergarten and
in elementary school, we crafted gifts for the mothers. From
sixth grade on, they planned competitions for girls and even
class discotheques, which we looked forward to so ardently.
After all, the boys in our class had received little tokens of
appreciation from the girls on Red Army Day, now it was
our turn to give gifts. That was the first time that we could
plan to give gifts without adult supervision. We collected 20
kopeks from each boy and went to a pharmacy. The shelves

were already partly swept clean, and there was not a great selection available anyway for our small change. Actually, we had no alternative and bought ten packages of soap. With the remaining money, we bought for each girl also a little comb with fine, thick teeth. We presented it together with the soap on the evening of the class disco. Of course we were rather disappointed about the girls' reaction. They not only refused to accept our presents but also declared that we would get the silent treatment for the evening. Only on the following day, could we make peace with each other again.

Despite the wilted carnations, despite many disappointments and misunderstandings, despite remarkable ideological incentives, we liked to celebrate March 8 and Soviet Army Day. These celebrations gave us an opportunity to learn how to deal with our sexuality and also to give each other tokens of consideration. Even though the combs that we unwittingly bought for the girls in our class for March 8 were lice combs.

Secret Easter Network

My grandmother would have made a good secret agent. We always marveled at her communications skills: Whenever a German came to our city, sooner or later he paid us a visit. We could have opened a Secret German Consulate in our apartment. Here news was discussed, German novels were exchanged, and often there was even singing. I liked guests very much and was glad to make the acquaintance of new people again and again at home. The secret network built up by my grandmother served not only to preserve German culture but also to celebrate Easter day correctly.

On the Soviet calendar, naturally, there were no religious holidays. Nevertheless, it was known when the Orthodox celebrated their Easter. For the Catholics, it was all much more complicated. Through her network, my grandmother sent in a roundabout way letters still written in Sütterlin [an old-fashioned cursive German script] to someone in Germany and months later received a reply with the dates of the Easter celebrations for the next five years. From the date of Easter, she then calculated all the other feasts in the Easter season and also the beginning of Lent and forwarded these dates to other interested parties. Then all was quiet for a few years, until the whole secret campaign started over from the beginning.

We almost always celebrated Easter twice: once according to the Catholic calendar and once according to the Orthodox. The Soviet regime had managed to erase almost all church holidays from people's consciousness. But it did not work with *Pascha* (that is the word for Easter in Russian, too).

Many Easter customs were kept and passed down from generation to generation. For example, there were several ways of dyeing eggs naturally. Eggs boiled in a brew made out of onion skins turn deep red. Part of Orthodox Easter was always *kulich*—a Russian Easter bread with raisins, vanilla, nutmeg, and a sugar glaze. You could even purchase such Easter loaves a few days before Easter in the government bakeries under the politically correct label of "Spring Cakes". Another tradition that survived all atheistic opposition is the Eastern greeting. "Christ is risen!" was the most common greeting on this day, even during the Soviet era. The response, "Truly He is risen!" could be heard in private circles even from Communists. But there was no Easter bunny in the Orthodox tradition. I was very happy, though, that the Easter bunny was Catholic and made his way to our city every year just for me. Once I managed to track down this rabbit: He was tall, had white hair and looked exactly like my grandmother. From that moment on, the mystery of Easter for me had nothing to do with the Easter bunny. The mystery of Easter is the Resurrection, which makes all things new. The Church had been declared dead back then, and the Christian holy days had fallen into oblivion, but their revival speaks for itself.

Instructive Bullfights

One of the most influential educators in the world is the street. On the street in our town, there was always a lot going on. Many parents let their children play until darkness fell, for there was not much crime and everything seemed safe. In the summer and even in the winter, we liked to spend our free time outdoors: playing, talking, arguing, and overstepping legal boundaries again and again. There were many boys and also various groups that liked to teach each other things that were not addressed in school or in the family.

I started smoking as early as first grade. A boy from another street informed me that cigarettes help you to grow up faster. I thought that was great, because grown-ups are allowed to go to sleep later, can eat lots of ice cream, and travel by train whenever they want. Andrei brought a cigarette with him, and I took my first puff. The smoke did not taste good at all, and I started to cough. It is not so easy after all to become a grown-up. Bravely I inhaled a second time. We made an appointment for the next day to continue our secret campaign. When we met again, though, there was no cigarette. Andrei walked through the streets and collected butts that were lying on the ground. I found those butts so unappetizing that I decided to wait a while until our science finally invented a tablet that will enable every child to grow up right away. So at the age of seven, I quit smoking, one day after I had started.

In fifth grade, I had found a new pal, who was very self-reliant and interesting. He had managed to skip school for several months in such a way that his parents did not notice it. He always had time for me and devised a new adventure for every meeting. One day, he persuaded me to skip school and, instead, to play the whole time with him. Everything went well, and it was relaxing. In the afternoon, we decided to imitate a Spanish bullfight. First, he was the bull, and I was the toreador. I had to excite him with my jacket and run away from him. We had a lot of fun and laughed a lot. Then we swapped roles. I bent my index fingers into horns, bowed my head, ran after him, and while doing so hit someone in the stomach. When I saw who was standing in front of me, I was speechless. It was our school principal, who was also my math teacher. "Excuse me, tomorrow I will come to school again", I said. "Then goodbye, and till tomorrow", Ludmila Pavlovna replied. At that moment it became quite clear to me that I had done something wrong. It was also very embarrassing for me to meet her the next day. I expected my fair punishment, but the teacher said nothing at all to me about our meeting the day before, which tormented my conscience much more. At the end of the school day, I waited for her beside the faculty lounge and said that I would never skip school again. "I see that you have understood everything, and I believe you. All the rest will be our secret", said Ludmila Pavlovna. Even when she left our school a year later, I kept my word until graduation. The street is one of the most influential teachers in the world. There you can learn very well to test your own limits and also to set them.

The Treasure of the *Titanic*

The doorbell rang. At the door stood a man in a suit who said, "Well, now, we have finally found you. A magnificent inheritance belongs to you." I once saw this scene in a movie and imagined that something like that would happen to us, too, someday. For I was waiting for the treasures of the *Titanic*. Actually the *Titanic* was very little known in the Soviet Union. Even my teacher may not have known what the *Titanic* was. For us, however, it remained a part of our family history that could no longer be verified.

My grandmother often told stories about her aunt, who lived in America and was very rich, since she owned a horse farm and a chocolate factory. Once this aunt came with her husband and children to Europe in order to visit her relatives, and while there she began to dream that the ship would sink on the return trip. These dreams occurred repeatedly and were so insistent that all her relatives knew about them. After long reflection, the family decided to exchange the tickets and to take the safest ship in the world—the *Titanic*. No one from her family was able to survive that voyage. My grandmother remembered very well condolence letters that her parents had preserved in a wooden frame.

I liked to listen when my grandmother told us something about our family history. She grew up in a German settlement in Russia. Until the moment when Communists came into her house one day, she had not spoken a word of Russian. For in the settlement, everything was just like in Germany—a German school, German physicians, a German Catholic Church, German merchandise. Even furniture, books, and tableware were shipped from Germany. Her stories about her childhood in a big house with a gigantic apple orchard sounded like a fairy tale. I found particularly fascinating a highly polished box that was decorated with angels, had a secret compartment, and could play music. These painted angels saved the lives of my grandmother and her three children, because during the war the music box was exchanged for a sack of potatoes.

The first of my ancestors came to Russia in the year 1798: the musician Matthias Graf. Before that, the Graf family had lived for generations in Worms [a city now in Rhineland-Palatinate]. Now the musician wanted to provide his family with a secure future and decided at the age of fifty-eight to start a new life in Russia. Our family tree includes many other families named Schulmeister, Brost, Herdle, Taylor, Rowein, Wiesner, and Ehrlich. Some came considerably later to Russia, many even just before the October Revolution. Afterward, there was no way back. My grandparents lived on the Black Sea in Novorossiysk, where my mother, too, was born in the year 1940. When the war started, she, like thousands of other German families, was forcibly deported to Kazakhstan. Grandfather Johannes Graf lost his life in 1942 in a concentration camp on account of his nationality. During the repressions, Grandma was under constant government surveillance and had to report daily with her three children to the commandant's office. Pursuant to the special ruling of the country's Supreme Tribunal, the family was assigned to Kazakhstan, not for a specified time, but for all eternity. After Stalin's death, fortunately, this eternity came to an end.

"When I look back," my grandmother said to me once, "our family history was like that of the *Titanic*. We wanted to get through life safely and all ended up in a catastrophe. Unlike many others, we survived it." Despite the difficulties, my grandma kept her sense of humor and an inexhaustible cheer until her final days. Often, though, she would break into tears, but tried again and again to regard the insane tragedy of her generation as a tragicomedy. The one thing that no Communists and no repressions could take from her was her faith. In order to believe, she needed no proof of God's existence, because He could be recognized clearly in the ups and downs of her life. The Christian faith, which overcomes all the defeats of life, was the real treasure that I, too, received as an inheritance.

Wanted: Heroes

After fifth grade, we received a homework assignment for the summer vacation. By September, everyone had to write an essay on the topic "The Destiny of the Family in the Destiny of the Country". In other words, we were supposed to seek information and report on the role that our grandparents and great-grandparents played during the Revolution, in the War, and in building up socialism. Most children could report proudly about their grandpas, since they were World War II veterans. Many could tell stories about their fathers, too, since they received awards as exemplary Communist workers. I wanted to tell something about my family, too, but did not know what. By then I was already aware that my mother's side of the family could not identify any heroes of socialism. So I tried to learn as much as possible about my grandparents on my father's side.

I began my family research in the library. The surname Krylov is not uncommon. It is the sixty-fourth on the list of popular Russian surnames. Especially well known in Russia is the author of fables Ivan Krylov, who came into the world exactly two hundred years before me and was the tsar's librarian. The name itself comes from *krylo*, which means "wing". Genealogists associate this name with the poor nobility and explain the derivation of the name in terms of intellectual tasks, ecclesiastical service, and church music. It was exciting information for me, but with a name and heritage like that, I could not get far in the workers' state. My only remaining hope was a conversation with my uncle in Moscow. He related that my father's family had lived for several generations before the October Revolution in the Khamovniki District in Moscow, in what is today the center of the city. Our ancestors were, among other things, judges, officials, and estate owners. When the Revolution began, my grandfather packed up his belongings and hid in a village near the old Russian city of Kostroma. He thereby secured for himself and his family not only freedom but also survival. All three of his children later moved back to Moscow. He himself died at the age of ninety-four in his village, shortly before I came into the world. To my disappointment (then), my grandpa was neither a war veteran nor an award-winning socialist worker.

Well, what was I supposed to write for this school composition? My mother's father died in a concentration camp as an enemy of the people, and the other grandfather came from the family of an estate owner and hid in the remote provinces so as to avoid contact with Communists as much as possible. Had this family contributed at least something to the destiny of socialism? Would our teacher say now that nothing could be expected of me, either? My good pal recommended that I make up a war story myself. "No one in Moscow is going to inquire about what your grandfather actually did." Relieved by such a simple solution, I began to write. But I did not write about wartime heroics; rather, I wrote about my mother, who had to work a lot so as to provide for me and my grandmother. I wrote that her simple humanity was just as important for the Communist future as her service at her workplace. One week after we had handed in our compositions, our teacher read some of them aloud to the class, praised others, and a few were even recommended for the school-wide competition. My text was not mentioned in this evaluation.

An Unknown Dimension

People often ask me whether as a child I already wanted to become a priest. My honest answer: It was entirely out of the question. Not because I found being a priest unattractive, but rather because I had never seen either a Catholic priest or a church. I first set foot in a Catholic church when I was twenty years old. For in our city there was no church. Only after *perestroika* did I discover a Catholic church in central Moscow—surrounded by KGB buildings. This Church of St. Louis later became my Christian home. In the Soviet era, we knew nothing at all about the existence of a Catholic church in Moscow. So we Catholics lived out our faith without the possibility of attending Mass or speaking with a priest. When a Catholic church could be seen incidentally in a film, my heart beat faster. It was an opportunity to come into contact with another hidden world. At that time, I even purchased a recording of organ music from the cathedral in Riga, Latvia, so as to able to imagine the Liturgy better. I had no idea what actually happens during Holy Mass.

A story about my uncle shows what an encounter with a priest could mean in those days. Uncle Willibald lived at the time in the large industrial city Chelyabinsk, where there was an unofficial German settlement. He was a very cautious, indeed, very shy man, who always tried to avoid all risk, even the slightest. Once he heard the whispered news that in the city there was a German Catholic priest secretly traveling through. Despite all the possible dangers, my uncle decided to speak with this priest.

Late in the evening, he went conspiratorially to a private residence at the city limits. In the residence there were a few other people who also wanted to speak to the priest. For each visitor, there was a quarter of an hour maximum. When it was my uncle's turn and he was alone with the priest in a room, he began to weep for happiness and excitement. Such an encounter was for many people not just an opportunity to see a representative of the Church, but rather confirmation that God had not abandoned them and had not forgotten them. Experiencing this divine consolation not only gave my rather reserved uncle a childlike joy but brought him to tears. The priest held my uncle's hand in his hands, and they sat beside each other that way, both weeping. The quarter hour was over quickly, and behind the door someone else was waiting, for whom every minute with the priest might be just as significant. None of our relatives knew about this encounter until the day on which I became a priest.

Why was it entirely out of the question for me as a child to become a Catholic priest? At that time, a Catholic priest did not belong to the dimensions of our real life. As a child, I wanted at one time to be a teacher, at others times to be a historian or a journalist. It was easier for me to imagine becoming a cosmonaut or a ballet dancer than a priest. The ways of the Lord are not only inscrutable but also full of adventures and surprises.

Goodbye, Lenin

Every Soviet citizen who had ever been in Moscow was asked by his acquaintances and colleague whether he had seen Lenin. The Lenin Mausoleum was not only the place most worth seeing but also the most important place of pilgrimage and the central cultic object in the country. The mausoleum building was designed by a former church architect according to all the rules of sacred structures. Poets and artists, kindergarten instructors and teachers, textbooks and newspapers—all agreed that visiting the mausoleum was not only a duty of gratitude to Lenin but also a ray of light in the brilliant future of our country.

Obviously I, too, wanted to see the light of the future and visit the genial Lenin in Moscow. Our family and our relatives plainly had had no particular interest in Lenin. Despite my regular stays in Moscow, my wish to visit Lenin had still not been granted. It was not easy, either, because the mausoleum was open only a few days a week and only a few hours a day. Millions of simple Soviet citizens came to Moscow to accomplish two goals—to see Lenin and to shop. Once my wish was fulfilled after all. At half past three in the night, we set out. When we got to the Alexander Gardens, the line of people looked endless. Had we arrived a half hour later, we would not even have been allowed to stand in line. While waiting for the doors to the mausoleum to open, I had lots of time to view the Kremlin wall and the people from all corners of the world.

At ten in the morning, the line began to move slowly. Everyone became serious and very quiet. The soldiers in the honor guard in front of the entrance to the mausoleum stood without making the slightest movement—here the boundary between life and death blurred, and something started that pointed the way into eternity. On the dark staircase leading down, one of the staff showed us which way to walk. I wanted to ask my mother something, but every noise and every word was immediately cut off. You were not allowed to talk or look around or stop. You were only allowed to look at Lenin and to move slowly in single file in a prescribed direction around the tomb to the exit. I tried to be as attentive as I could and to take note of everything exactly; after all, I had waited so long for this moment. But in no way whatsoever did I have a sense of joy. Instead, this sacred stillness had an intimidating and even somewhat sinister effect on me. These few minutes spent with Lenin underground seemed very long to me, so that I was happy and relieved to see the sunlight again. Quickly and quietly we walked past the tombs of the Soviet statesmen and began to speak only after we left Red Square.

At that time, I could not answer the question of whether I liked the mausoleum. I was rather disappointed, for instead of a symbol of the brilliant future of our country, I had got to see only a dark room with a shriveled corpse. Several years later, as I was writing my doctoral dissertation, I had the privilege of getting even more closely acquainted with Lenin and of viewing his brain in the Institute for Brain Research. Shortly after his death, this brain was cut into slices for research purposes, in order to reveal to the world the secrets of Lenin's genius. For millions of people, Lenin became an idol who deserves eternal veneration and supposedly leads them into a brilliant future. As a child, I had no way of suspecting that only ten years later so many people would share my impression of the mausoleum. For every idol always leaves the same legacy—disappointment.

The War for Peace

If I were to calculate the number of hours spent on social activism during my school years, then first place would go, not to works that benefit the public, like collecting waste paper and scrap metal, not to conservation, and not to ideological training, but rather to our fight for peace and the brotherhood of peoples. After three months of summer vacation, the school year for all schoolchildren throughout the country began on the same day: September 1. And the first period of instruction was always about peace. The best students had the honor of reciting poems about peace, and in the upper grades they would read aloud newspaper reports from the war-torn regions of the world. Often these peace lessons were genuinely alarming for us children; there was no denying the message: The future of the earth is in great danger. We can save the world from a global catastrophe only if every single one of us stands up for peace and friendship among nations.

Even though we often tuned out the news about the successes of the socialist country, we found the fight for peace enormously important. Without questioning the cause, I gladly fought for peace, as long as this fight consisted of drawing on the streets with chalk, folding Origami paper cranes, and playtime. Then there were the annual competitions: "The Red Star" for correct marching and "The Red Carnation" for the best-performed songs. In the last two

87

grades, we also had to demonstrate our capabilities by taking apart and reassembling a Kalashnikov [assault rifle]. No one noticed that all these activities were not particularly peaceful. On the peace posters, you could see machine guns, ammunition, or imperialists sitting on a bomb. Of course, in presenting the peace texts, the reader made a particularly serious and sullen face. During the peace ceremonies, we often wore a homemade military uniform and thus became little soldiers in the war for peace.

The activities promoting friendship among peoples were somewhat friendlier. At the concerts entitled "Fifteen Republics—Fifteen Sisters", each class was supposed to present the folklore of one of the Soviet Republics. Particularly exciting were our theatrical productions about friendship with African countries. Although most of us had never seen someone with dark skin, nevertheless, every boy wanted to portray an African and have his face painted with soot. Since I liked to take an interest in all social activities, I decided to become involved in the cause of friendship among peoples, too.

In our neighborhood lived Ukrainians, White Russians, Jews, Bashkirs, Tatars, Mari, Latvians; across the hall from us lived a Tatar family. In order to bring friendship among people to our apartment building, I decided to learn Tatar and in the future to greet our neighbors only in their mother tongue. Kolya from our class had learned a few Tatar words from his grandmother and said that he was willing to teach me the language. I collected on a piece of paper the most important sentences or sayings, and he wrote the translation of each for me. "The Tatar language is very compact", I thought when I saw the paper. Every sentence was translated with only one word. I went to Erik, who like Kolya was from a Bashkir-Tatar family. He was offended by my friendly

"Good day" and replied, "You yourself are a dog." When I showed him my list, he determined that Kolya probably wanted to hide the fact that he had no command whatsoever of his mother tongue. During the holidays, his grandmother taught him words for animals, and he wrote these down on my paper. If I had tried to use this vocabulary to speak with my neighbors, I would have said "cow" instead of "thank you", "cat" instead of *Gesundheit* [when someone sneezed], and "goat" instead of "goodbye". I think that they would not have held it against me. Moreover, I was willing to teach Kolya a few German words, but he decided to learn his Tatar language first. I cannot say whether our fight for peace bore fruit, but our friendship between peoples did.

The Mobile Confessional

Often I used to count the days until vacation, for we often traveled then, and I could hardly wait to ride the train again. In those days, the train took thirty-four hours to make a 1,240-mile trip by rail. It was not in the least bit boring. Forests, hills, rivers, little wooden villages, and again woods, valleys, hills, fields, and villages. At the stations, you could buy something to eat through the train window from local *babushkas*. At one station, they still sold hot boiled potatoes and pickled cucumbers; at another—dried fish or local cherries, pears, apples, and tomatoes; in other words, regional specialties. At the major stations, the train stopped for fifteen to twenty minutes. During this time, the conductors knocked on the wheels to test them, while the passengers had the opportunity to run quickly to the train station to get ice cream or even sometimes fresh kefir. The food brought along from home—usually hardboiled eggs, pickles, and roast chicken—was usually shared with other passengers.

Each car had its own conductress, who not only checked the tickets but also cleaned the car, maintained order, and several times a day brought to each compartment hot tea with individually wrapped sugar cubes. While eating, all the fellow travelers got into a conversation. Since the chances of meeting someone again in this gigantic country were very slim, people told each other the stories of their lives. For some individuals, this sort of train trip was like a confession. They confided mistakes for which forgiveness alone was not enough, mistakes that people still regretted and dragged along with them through their lives. So the passengers chatted with each other about their secret sins, worries, and fears and hoped to find peace for their souls through the approval of their fellow travelers.

When I was in sixth grade, I convinced my mother to let me ride alone for a trip from Moscow to the Ural region. My aunt brought me into the train compartment and asked the conductress and the passengers to take care of me. I quickly became acquainted with all my fellow travelers and felt qualified to participate in the confidential conversations of the adults. They spoke about love, treachery, betrayal, and hope. "I threatened to kill him if he looks at another woman again. Since then everything at home has been fine", one self-assured fellow traveler ended her account.

I, too, wanted to contribute something confidential, but at the age of twelve, my life experience was too meager. Then the idea occurred to me to relate something that I was not allowed to talk about with my school friends. I thought about engravings from Grandma's books and began to speak as well as I could about the faith. Most people then had never seen a Bible in their whole life, and they had no idea whatsoever about biblical stories. So to the astonishment of the grown-ups, I told them about Cain and Abel, about Noah's Ark, about Abraham and Moses, and obviously about Jesus. My fellow travelers marveled about the secrets of the Bible that I confided to them. I even gave to one young lady our private address, so that she could send me a recipe for her delicious "Napoleon" cake. That was very reckless of me, because with my name and address, she could have alerted the school about my religious views. In a letter that I in fact received from her two weeks later, she wrote that she was thinking about our conversation and sent me the desired recipe. Our attempt to make the "Napoleon" cake did not succeed, but my first solo trip was a memorable one and even had no negative consequences. After all, there was a similarity between confidential train conversations and confession—the secrecy.

The Artistic Sacrifice

My primary authority in the realm of art and culture was Aunt Taya—an elderly lady who lived in our apartment house. She herself had no doubt that she was living out her calling: "Be glad that people like me are active in cultural matters; otherwise, what would happen to our society . . . ?" Aunt Taya worked in the municipal cultural palace as a cleaning woman. She had a lot of clout there, because in those days a good cleaning woman was not at all easy to find. Her importance for art and culture was almost proverbial. Even when admission tickets were sold for plays, concerts, or circuses, she could always find a seat for me, usually for free. Often she herself stood at the door checking tickets.

So for me, at first, my whole cultural life played out in our cultural palace. It was one of the most beautiful buildings in our city. The ceiling of the foyer was painted like the sky, in which pilots and parachutists could be seen. A gigantic chandelier hung in the auditorium, and the walls were decorated with pictures of representatives of various professions. On one bas-relief over the main entrance, a quotation from Lenin could be read: "Culture belongs to the people."

The culture that belonged to the people consisted mainly of amateur performances—concerts and emotional literature readings. For the good of the people, businesses and professional groups were obliged to practice choral works or dances and to perform them in public. Some sang about

Lenin and the Revolution, others presented melancholy folk songs about nature or lamented unrequited love. In school, too, we sang about love: about love for our homeland and for the Communist Party. The teachers were responsible for our cultural activities as well and after the day's lessons had to practice various scenes with us. The uncomplicated melodies of the patriotic tunes, which were surprisingly similar to recent German liturgical songs, supposedly testified to the closeness of the music to the simple people.

The meaning of all these activities became clear to me through a framed inscription that hung in our cultural palace: "Art demands sacrifice. K. Stanislawski." I could interpret what that was supposed to mean from various perspectives. We learned that Communists sacrifice their lives for our future, that the heroes of labor devote their strength so that we might lead a carefree life. So I could understand that something was being asked of me, too, now. Patiently watching amateur performances for hours was for me, at any rate, a sacrifice that Soviet art demanded of me.

On the other hand, I got an entirely different impression in the theaters, exhibitions, and museums in Moscow. The first time I went to the theater, I saw the adult drama *Maria Stuart* by Friedrich Schiller. I certainly did not understand it all, but the theater impressed me so much that to this day I can still recall individual scenes. At the age of thirteen or fourteen, we learned to distinguish between official and unofficial art. Some plays could be seen on television, but others were circulated through semi-legal channels and private tape recordings. The official performances had to correspond to the spirit of the people and were often approved by special artistic committees. Rebellious artists were morally condemned and could count on being shunned publicly by their colleagues. Here the inscription "Art demands sacrifice" acquired its broader meaning.

Quite obviously our local creative types sacrificed themselves for art—for example, the accordion player from the municipal cultural palace. One morning he was found sleeping in the practice room. Since his wife did not believe in her husband's sacrificial devotion, he had to spend the night on chairs. The poor musician had practiced until late at night with his amateur group, and only on the way home did he notice that he did not have his scarf with him. He went back and, without turning the overhead light on, took something out of the artists' wardrobe and wrapped it around his neck. His wife was already waiting for him at the door to the house and could not understand why her husband had had to work so late. The explanation took a new turn when the accordion player took off his coat. Around his neck was wrapped a pink skirt which normally female dancers wear. In the following days, only the intervention of his colleagues could calm the jealous woman somewhat and help to reconcile the family. The accordion player no doubt saw himself as a true victim of art. What other sacrifices did the art in our cultural palace demand? The answer remains hidden from history at first.

Conscious Discipline

We had a lot of respect for our school principal and were even a bit afraid of her. She was a staunch Communist, but also an intelligent and conscientious woman. Although the social conditions in our school were by no means easy, she managed to establish not only order but also a collective consciousness. An important concept for this purpose was so-called conscious discipline. We learned to love and to cultivate our school as well as our socialist country, not out of duty, but rather out of interior conviction. Our principal tried to achieve this by innovative measures.

One day, the whole school was suddenly assembled. The principal's voice sounded as though the next World War had broken out. Something terrible had happened—someone had forgotten to flush the toilet, and, to make matters worse, there was litter on the floors of the school. We had to learn to consider our school, not as a public building, but as our common house. Several years after graduation, this principal admitted to me that often during classes she herself would scatter wads of paper on the floors so as to observe during recess which students or even teachers would walk past them. Conscious discipline meant that we ourselves noticed all the defects in the school and were also supposed to remedy them. In order to foster conscious discipline, there were even days of self-management in our school. Once a year, all the teachers were locked into the faculty lounge and all the positions in the school were taken over by us students. The students taught, gave each other homework, and graded the results. Even the principal and all other school administrators were appointed from among the students on that day. We liked those days very much and took our responsibility seriously.

The problem with conscious discipline was actually a relevant one throughout the country. When the government treats its citizens like children, these citizens then behave like children, too. Discipline at work, quality of work, and punctuality had become an insoluble problem of the socialist system. They tried to solve it with campaigns like "The Five-Year Plan of Quality and Efficiency" or with surprise discipline checks. Even as students, we already got an inkling of this in school.

At this point, I must admit that I have always had a problem with punctuality. The problem was that I was always punctual and therefore constantly had to wait for others. My friends often told me that I, too, should arrive later. It was somehow difficult for me, though, to understand why I should arrive later when a particular time had been agreed on. In all of my years in school, I never overslept and never was late. There was only one single exception: during recess, I went to the schoolyard as usual and there met the teacher of our class, who wanted to tell me something. I did not consider it polite to interrupt the teacher and remained with her another five minutes after the school bell rang. At the entrance to the school, our school patrol stopped me and marked me down as tardy. Since that day had been declared the day for the Discipline and Order Campaign, I was specially portrayed on a cartoon. Under a picture with a disorderly student was the following caption: "Shame! Such students always arrive too late and slow down our learning process. Let's teach him what order means!'' I had no opportunity to explain my situation to anyone: When the education of the collective was at stake, everything else was unimportant. It is also difficult to say whether this cartoon contributed anything to the conscious discipline in our school and to my conscious discipline. At any rate, it taught me to take societal campaigns more seriously.

I learned a form of conscious discipline from my mother, without calling it that. Not only because she herself had one, but also because she also gave me her unlimited trust. As a little child, I already knew where all our savings were hidden at home, and I never thought of taking any of it. Moreover, my mother never checked my homework. She said that she trusted me and that I was big enough to understand the importance of homework assignments. I was allowed to stay overnight with friends whenever I wanted and, once I was a teenager, had no curfew. She obviously cared about me and never went to sleep before I had come back home. For my mother's educational method was trust and freedom, the unmistakable expression of great love.

My Double Life

One evening, my mother came home somewhat concerned. After dinner, she asked me to give her advice as to what methods she should use to raise me. Her female coworker had told her that my development was a cause for great concern. All normal children my age used to play soccer and cards, work in the garden, plant potatoes, or go fishing. I, on the other hand, spent my time irresponsibly and wasted it on books. This coworker warned my mother that she should reconsider how she was raising me, because books are dangerous. Therefore, if my mother did not urgently take control of my development, I might ruin my whole life.

The attentive coworker had noticed something that the school had not recorded at first. At the age of around eleven, I began my double life. In our society, school and fun did not go together. The important thing was to reproduce the contents of the textbooks, if possible verbatim. Scientific subjects took up a great part of our classroom hours. But my favorite subject was history. This way I could gain knowledge about the Church and about the faith that otherwise would be secret, and I even resolved to become a history teacher after graduation.

From fifth grade on, there was foreign language instruction at school for two hours a week, and we could choose between German and English. Especially important in learning foreign languages were ideological texts. For example,

I could recite by heart in German the biographies of Karl Marx, Ernst Thälmann, and Clara Zetkin and also report at length on how the Young Pioneers collected scrap metal and waste paper. In 1991, when I went to Germany for the first time through the Gorbachev-Kohl youth exchange program, I found out that no one was interested in the activities of the Young Pioneers.

Since rote learning was never my forte—from my perspective at the time, it was often senseless—sometimes I would put aside my homework assignments and disappear into another world. This world was the library. In our little city, there were four libraries—a children's library, a young people's library, a central library, and a union library. The last-mentioned was especially well stocked with about 100,000 books and became my second home. As time went on, I was treated there almost like a grown-up coworker. I helped the librarians with their duties and in return had the run of the place. I was allowed to remain in the library even outside of the regular times, to spend hours in otherwise locked storerooms of books and to read books from special collections.

In the library, I became acquainted with many other children and was even appointed the chairman of the young bibliophiles' club that we founded. We organized readings, book displays, and literature evenings, we playacted and brought special books to workplaces and union meetings. I learned to write a literary Russian style and to speak in public. The most fascinating thing, though, was the universe that I discovered in books: first, the adventure stories by Alexander Dumas, Jules Verne, Jack London; later on, the deep, religious-philosophical works by Fyodor Dostoyevsky, Anton Chekov, and Mikhail Bulgakov, and furthermore all sorts of popular scientific books and encyclopedias. When

I first understood what sorts of things could be discovered in an encyclopedia, I looked up Vatican City. In school or in the media, nothing was ever said about the Vatican, so that I was not sure whether the little Catholic state from our private conversations existed at all. I was overjoyed that the *Great Soviet Encyclopedia* not only confirmed the existence of the Vatican and the pope, but also revealed that besides us there were millions of other Catholics in the world.

Now I became acquainted with my new friends, with whom I got along well, not on the street, but in books. The heroes in the novels were adventuresome and could make honest, courageous decisions. They seemed quite different from the people all around me. I used every opportunity to read: during recess, in bed, while taking walks, and in other places. The deeper I became immersed in world literature and in the search for the meaning of existence, the more I distanced myself from school. On the one hand, the library offered me a flight from reality into a world of free thinking; on the other hand, I actually began to doubt whether I would make it to graduation and someday find a place in life. Our geography teacher said in front of the whole class that uneducated people like me would interfere with the building up of Communism. The chemistry teacher thought that I was incapable of study and would never be admitted to the polytechnic. From her perspective, my good grades at the university and my later scientific research can only be described as a miracle. My mother's attentive coworker was right—books are dangerous; they can mislead you to reflect and lead to surprising changes in life.

Harmful Chewing Gum

I cannot recall exactly whether it was the same with the girls, but a simple piece of chewing gum was enough to make us boys enthusiastic. For until then, we had seen chewing gum only in the movie theater. Through our acquaintances, I tried Western chewing gum again and again and shared it with friends. Our boys then lent these sticks of chewing gum to others: Each one was allowed to chew for a few minutes. Those who were not so fortunate tried it with tar and bitumen. It was just cool to chew, like in the movies. I would probably have forgotten these experiences if they had not taught me a lesson in school.

It is good to share, regardless of whether you yourself have a lot or a little—I learned this simple rule not only in our Christian home but also in school. I always thought that sharing is good. When I saw the first Soviet chewing gum for the first time in Moscow in the supermarket, I immediately bought several packs, so as to share them with my pals. A white pack with an orange-colored label: *Aphelsino-vaya* (orange-flavored) contained five sticks. I brought several packs with me to school and shared them during recess with my fellow students. People today can only imagine the feelings of the teacher who came into the class afterward. Never in her life had she herself seen chewing gum before, and at first she could not cope with us chomping, lip-smacking boys. When she finally determined that we were doing something that was supposedly foreign to a Soviet student on principle, she folded a bag out of the newspaper and walked down the rows with it. None of us wanted to spit out his long-desired chewing gum, but the teacher's serious glare told us that all resistance was futile.

Over the next few weeks, several explanatory talks were given at school. They even invited a professional from the local health inspector's office to tell us hair-raising stories about chewing gum. Chewing gum would corrode our stomachs from within and lead to a disproportionate development of the jaws, as in horses. The main danger of chewing gum, however, lay in the intentions of the capitalists. We were told that they had devised special kinds of chewing gum to endanger Soviet children or even to poison them. The fact that the chewing gum that I distributed had been produced in Moscow made no difference. Several years later, it was permissible and possible to buy chewing gum everywhere in our town, too, and all the excitement over it was forgotten. For me, it was certainly good to learn that the decisive thing in sharing is not the action but the contents.

The Forbidden Book

In the Soviet Union, it was self-evident that you would have a negative opinion about something that disagreed with the Party line, regardless of whether you had read, seen, or heard it. With certain views, everyone knew from the start what was good and what was not. For example, there was a book that only a few people were allowed to read, but everyone was supposed to criticize. That was the Bible. When my family was deported, my grandparents were allowed to take with them only what they could carry in their own hands. And so among other things, they brought along three prayer books and a short Bible history for Catholic elementary schools. Even though I could not read these books, which were printed in Fraktur [traditional Gothic] type, they were for me a true testimony of the faith. The children's book with the Bible stories made me curious about the Bible. But none of our neighbors or my school friends owned one.

Finally, in the library, I discovered two atheistic books: *The Bible for Believers and Unbelievers* and *The Amusing Gospel*. In both books, the Christian faith was mocked and refuted, which was nothing new to me. One discovery was that by reading between the lines, I could learn what actually is in the Bible. *The Amusing Gospel* related how stupid the family and followers of Jesus were; it told of how in His first miracle Jesus made wine out of water because of His own predilection for alcohol, or how at the Last Supper He instituted a pedicure. In this book, though, there was something valuable, too. At the beginning of each new chapter, you could read the original texts from the Gospel. The librarian at that time had allowed me to practice typing on a typewriter. "Eureka!" I thought, and took this mockery of the Bible with me to type for myself a copy of all the Bible citations. This secret mission lasted several weeks, because at that time I could type with only one finger. The risk was not in vain; at the conclusion, I owned several pages with my own edition of the Gospel. It was really the first time in my life that I published a book.

The first publicly accessible Bible was not printed until the year 1990. I waited then at the door of the bookstore for it and spent a month's wages on it. The prohibition against owning a Bible in the Soviet Union could only confirm its importance. The Communists feared that a freely accessible Bible might make believers out of Soviet atheists. And they were right.

Rotten Protests

For many people, it is hard to imagine, but there were protests in the Soviet Union, too. As schoolchildren, we even took part in such protests. If the future of the planet was at stake, it was very important to raise your voice and to proclaim societal positions publicly. Since the Soviet country needed well-educated individuals, the protests were only rarely allowed during the school day. It was a shame, since it is fun demonstrating instead of sitting in class.

There was, however, an essential difference between socialist protests and protests in Western democracies. In the West, people were dispersed with water cannons and tear gas. Our socialist protests were always supported by our media and our politics. The newspapers and those in government praised the active stance of the students and even took note of our opinions in the future programs. The success of our protests was shown, not by how we protested, but by what we protested against. Thus we liked to protest against the exploitation of children in capitalistic countries, against American arms manufacturers, and against the austerity policies of Margaret Thatcher; we protested for peace on earth, for the future of our planet, and for the freedom of political prisoners somewhere in the world. For us, protesting against our own government or against the Communist Party was out of the question. It would have been socially irresponsible, since we knew that all our happiness and the future of the earth lay in the hands of this Party, to which we should be infinitely grateful.

Our protests most commonly took the form of signature drives, poster contests, rallies, or sometimes even campaigns to recycle paper or other valuable materials. When the media reported again on the danger facing the world, we cut suitable peace appeals out of the newspaper and started little groups. Wearing serious, self-assured expressions, we went from door to door collecting signatures under the newspaper appeals. At the time, no one thought to ask what would happen to these signatures afterward. To this day, I have not learned the answer. We were especially happy when many rallies were organized directly in the school. Our activists could then give their resolute speeches for as long as they wanted; the main thing was that we missed one lesson or another.

I remember particularly well our protests against the British government and the related campaign in support of the mineworkers' strike in Great Britain. With the help of our teacher, we graphically imagined how bad off the poor British children must be now that their otherwise destitute parents had no work. We even had a guilty conscience because in the Soviet Union we had it so good, while the English children had to suffer. Together with thousands of Soviet students, we had decided to collect school supplies and toys for the poor British children. For this collection campaign, I gave away my own building blocks and was very happy to be able to make my contribution to justice in the world.

Then there was a comment once by Uncle Zakhar. That was my name for a watchman who was employed at my mother's workplace. Sometimes I found his statements funny without being able to understand their meaning. When I proudly told him about my building blocks for the English children, he set aside his newspapers, poured his strong tea, and said: "Look, boy, when the protests are supported by the government and are praised by their media—then there is something rotten about it."

The Specter of "We"

What we as children could not learn at home and on the street, we learned in summer camp. For most parents, it was possible to send their children to camp for four weeks during the summer vacation at almost no cost. For the children, this was an adventure in independent living; for the counselors, it was an opportunity to teach us a sense of "we". Personalities no longer existed at summer camp; there was only "we". What was adventurous in this sort of camp was precisely the tension between collective pressure and an almost military daily routine, on the one hand, and the desire for freedom, independence, and self-affirmation, on the other.

Our camp "Oak Grove" could accommodate around three hundred children at a time and consisted of a complex of six wooden barracks, a two-story center with movie theater, canteen, library and game rooms, a first-aid station, and a farmyard. Up to the age of ten, girls and boys were housed together in a large room with thirty beds; from age eleven onward, the girls and boys slept separately. Upon our arrival, we were divided up into groups of thirty children each and from that moment on did everything together under the supervision of a female counselor and a male Pioneer leader. Right on the first day, we went together to be weighed. Since not all children were fed well in their families, it was important at the end of the stay to report how many pounds each group was able to gain collectively. Once a week, the children marched to the farmyard to shower together in the public baths under the supervision of the adults. There was no privacy even there.

Patriotic music can arouse very special feelings in everyone when it blares from the loudspeakers on the street at seven o'clock in the morning and summons you out of a warm bed into the cool morning air. After morning gymnastics, we had fifteen minutes for personal hygiene. A latrine and a cold water pipe, along which dozens of spigots were attached, were found in the meadow. Before breakfast, all the groups of children and adolescents had roll call and rattled off their lines as they repeated the greeting. Before noon, the children cleaned their dormitories and play rooms and prepared the evening program. You could also find a little free time then. After the midday meal, there was an obligatory nap for two hours. In the evening, all the children met either at the woodland stage or in the movie theater. There were various competitions, theatrical presentations, homemade comedy sketches, as well as movie evenings and discotheques. At nine o'clock in the evening, when the children were in bed, the counselors told fairy tales, anecdotes, and often horror stories, too. The adolescents did not have to go to bed until 10:30. It was especially adventurous to leave the room at night through the window and to meet in a secret place. The more they controlled us and threatened us with punishments, the more enticing it was to test our own bravery. The hooting and screeching of owls sounded even weirder after the horror stories. Only the bad luck of being caught by one of the counselors after such a nocturnal excursion seemed to be worse than any monster.

Once all the boys agreed to stage a night of horror for the girls. Covered with white bed sheets like ghosts, we went very quietly at night into the girls' room, took up our positions beside the beds, and began to make spooky noises. What happened next sent most of us fleeing in a shameful panic. Our female counselor was lying in one of the beds. The girls had been restless in the evening, and so she remained that night in the girls' room to sleep there. When she saw us, she began scolding and screaming. Two pals and I managed to hide under a bed. For a long time, we lay motionless on the cold floor and feared that our racing heartbeat might betray us. Hiding brought us no advantages, though, because in the morning all the boys received a collective punishment. Even in disobedience, we all learned to decide collectively and to take responsibility as a collective also. When it came to the sense of "we", thinking and deciding for yourself was not necessary at all.

A few years later, we had to struggle in school with the *Manifesto of the Communist Party*. It famously begins with the sentence: "A specter is haunting Europe—the specter of Communism." Arguably, we saw that specter.

Levi's Jeans

It was not uncommon for fashion and consumption to be denounced in the Soviet Union as a weakness of immature, narrow-minded, bourgeois people. But the more they talked to Soviet youth about socialist ideals, the more these young people became interested in fashionable goods. For many of them, American brand-name jeans were at the pinnacle of all possible material desires. As soon as someone owned a pair of genuine American jeans, he was considered successful and enjoyed special attention from the girls. If you had good connections then, you could get a pair of Indian or Polish jeans in the big cities, but the American brands could not be found. In the provinces, jeans played no major role at first.

I was thirteen when Aunt Maria bought me my first pair of jeans in Moscow. I have no idea how she managed it, but they were genuine Levi's jeans. I could well imagine that this piece of clothing was something special, but as yet I had no idea about jeans. Before then, I had never heard the word Levi's and pronounced it as you would in German. Moreover, the coveted garment was too big. My mother suggested leaving the jeans in the wardrobe for the time being and waiting about a year until they fit me, but I did not bother to answer her. Who would wait that long? Besides, recently it had become noticeably harder to deal with the boys on our street who were going through puberty. I had hoped that my new garment would help win me additional respect in these rivalries. In order to make the jeans a little smaller, we washed them in hot water. Then I rolled up the cuffs a good eight inches, and went outdoors. My new clothes did not go unnoticed, and right away I was badly ridiculed. Everyone thought that my "overalls" were shabby and silly. They said that even the pajamas worn in kindergarten would be better for a teenager. None of these guys had even seen a pair of jeans before, and no one knew that they were actually in great demand. For me, these comments were unexpected and so disappointing that I did not want to go back home again. For a long while, I walked aimlessly through the city.

When it was already late, a group of older students and young adults walked up to me. They asked me whether what they saw was a pair of genuine jeans. Now, suddenly, I was at the center of enthusiastic attention. They even offered me money if I was willing to cut off the Levi's label and sell it. And so my jeans had regained their respectability on the same evening. For me, it was surely good to observe that respect for a pair of jeans was not respect for me and that clothes and people have different values. Even though I gave it no thought at first, my jeans proved that it takes a certain amount of courage to try something new.

Learning to Flirt

We got our first tip on flirting in school from our Russian teacher. The worst thing that could happen to you at your first meeting with a girl, Anna Ivanovna said, was grammatical errors, for instance, in the declensions of nouns. That would be a fiasco for every one of you. No girl would want to meet such a young man. Therefore, if you do not learn Russian, you will remain single your whole life and die alone. Then there will be no one to hand you a glass of water on your deathbed. It sounded very convincing. But instead of learning declensions, we began to look for additional tips on encounters between the sexes. It was not a question of sex at all, but rather of generally dealing with girls. In puberty, you begin to learn anew how to address a girl or to carry her schoolbag home for her.

In seventh grade, my pals and I definitely wanted to see a new film, but admission was for age sixteen and over. At that time, I wore my hair like the Beatles, a so-called "mushroom haircut", shoes with raised heels, and a trendy shirt with a big collar. We tried to make our voices sound deeper and pretended to be sixteen-year-olds. Some of us had no luck, but without further ado, I succeeded in getting past the ticket-taker. On a big screen, a young man kissed his girlfriend, and later on she told him that she was pregnant. That was enough not only to prohibit the film for children

but also to give wings to our imagination. Some boys spec-
ulated that a girl could become pregnant through kissing
alone. In those days, not one of us would have ventured to
give a girl a little kiss anyway.

Since we had no sex education in school, no one informed
us about the physiological processes of sexual relations. We
imagined these relations as a secret mystery that can develop
only from the love between a man and a woman. It was also
clear to us why no one talked about the subject—secrets are
secrets only if they are treated confidentially. Today many
people smirk at such notions about sex; however, they were
to be found not only among young people but also among
adults. In big cities, you could encounter just about anything
even then, but in the provinces, the mere word "lovers" was
often enough to make girls or even some women blush.

Right after the October Revolution, many social experi-
ments were conducted in Russia. There were even plans to
abolish the family completely as a relic of bourgeois narrow-
mindedness. As time went on, even the Communists understood that no society can have a future without the family
made up of father, mother, and children. Families were declared a cell of socialist society, and, consequently, morality
was raised to the status of a component of the "moral code
of a builder of Communism". This was meant seriously, as
shown by the case of our neighbor who married a Communist man. A few years later, when he left his wife for another
woman, she reported him to his Party cell. After an enlightening conversation with the comrade, the man returned to
his family. Only after the collapse of the Soviet Union did
we learn that two-timing was commonplace even among
Soviet politicians. In our circle, we never talked about sex
but always about love. Today's sex educators will scarcely

believe it, but all my pals, even without instructions from sex-ed class, managed not only to learn to flirt but also to start families and even to beget children. I cannot tell how helpful correct grammatical declensions may have been to them in accomplishing this.

Compelling Evidence

With the onset of puberty, many boys in our class became aggressive and tried on every occasion to prove themselves. No one could deal with it, neither they themselves nor their parents nor the school. Many came from so-called "difficult families" in which alcohol or domestic violence was an everyday reality. After school, these youngsters waited outside and selected a victim to beat or humiliate. It seemed pointless to go to the teachers for help, because they, too, were afraid of our classmates. Anything could happen: sometimes during class a dishrag flew toward our female teacher or a water balloon burst in front of the blackboard. I had no father, no older brother, and no one else who could protect me, but somehow I was always able to get home unharmed. It was as though I had a magic hat, and they could not see me at all after school.

Once, though, I was stopped in front of the school. The guys said that in two days I, too, should beat a boy of my choosing and in that way prove my masculinity. I asked my neighbor Edik to teach me boxing in those two days. When the day arrived, I chose as my victim a defenseless boy of the same age and waited together with the others until he left the school building. They all stood in a circle around us. I insulted my victim in a loud voice and was about to hit him. But when I looked him in the eyes, I turned around and ran away. It was embarrassing. I knew that my name, translated from Greek, is "defender", and yet, instead of defending others, I had been ready to hit a defenseless classmate. At the same time, I was very grateful to God that He had kept me from brawling. I did not know how I should apologize to that youngster. The next day at the school cafeteria, I bought a sweet pastry and offered him half of it. He took the half without saying a word. On that day, we walked home together after school. Even though no friendship resulted from it, we could nevertheless live together in peace.

One year later, on a dark evening, I was punched in the face. When I stood up again with a bloody nose, no one could be seen. It may be that someone had just given proof of his masculinity, with my participation. By no means do I want to give the impression with stories like this that our life as teenagers was dangerous. You just had to learn that this world is not inhabited exclusively by angels. Only once did I get into a serious situation. In an unfamiliar district, I was stopped by a dozen youths. Their facial expressions and body language showed that they were up to no good. The leader asked me what I was doing in his territory and whether I knew what I could expect as a result. There were no adults nearby, and unfortunately it was already too late to run away. Without reflecting, I made the sign of the cross and said in a loud voice: "God save and protect me!" This reaction of mine was not only unexpected but also dumbfounding for everyone, myself included. Certainly the guys had never seen and never heard such a thing and did not know how to deal with it. "Something is not right here. Let's go", the leader said, and at that moment I remained completely alone on the street. They say that God saves us from all danger and puts oppressors to flight, but I myself had not thought that invoking Him would have such a surprising effect. Now there is compelling evidence of it.

But No Kissing

Whereas German youngsters and teenagers in the 1980s read *Bravo* magazine, young Soviets had only the periodicals entitled *Flame* or *Pioneer*. But among Soviet teenagers, too, there was an interest in looking at color photos of pretty girls. Once, when I was visiting a pal, I found under his bed a notebook with black-and-white photos of Samantha Smith pasted into it.

Samantha was an American girl who had written a letter to the General Secretary of the Communist Party in Moscow in which she expressed her fear about the future of the world. She was invited to the Soviet Union and rapidly became a political star. All the news programs and all the papers told of how a simple girl summoned the courage to contradict adult rulers. Everyone talked about how she had made her way across the ocean in order to find out the truth and to save the world from a global catastrophe. For Soviet propaganda, Samantha was an unexpected gift. We students wanted to be like her; we wanted to demonstrate our active stance in life and to advocate peace throughout the world. Thus a young American girl became for many of us a heroine, and the most important thing was that she was just like us.

When Samantha died in 1985 in a plane crash, a Russian alternative was found to replace her. Katya Lycheva wrote a letter to U.S. President Ronald Reagan and was invited to the

United States. It seems that young girls produce good results for the political purposes of the various parties, whether or not they themselves notice it. You cannot be against, much less fight against, someone who is childlike, innocent, and also female. These experiences of Soviet ideology can be applied successfully today, too, if one wants to popularize certain political ideas in a clever way. In order to capitalize on young people's altruism, it is enough to make an icon out of a simple girl. When my pal admitted to me that he liked Samantha, I asked him confidentially whether he would kiss her if he ever got the opportunity. His indignant answer: "You idiot, how could I kiss a girl like that. After all, she is fighting for our future!"

Fabulous Communism

That summer evening, we gathered in the courtyard of our high-rise apartment complex. We chatted about life and started a conversation about our dreams and goals. At age thirteen, you already become more realistic and no longer plan to become a sea captain, treasure hunter, or cosmonaut. Some wanted to continue the steelworker dynasty of their family; others thought it would be super to drive a truck. With regard to our future, we were modest and optimistic at the same time. "I look forward most of all to having a real chance to experience Communism", Vova said. "It would be cool not to have to wait long for it", the others agreed. For many people, something better than Communism was almost unimaginable. If so many human beings have given everything and ultimately their life for Communism, then this desired future must be magnificent.

Many simple people imagined Communism as heaven on earth. For the theoreticians of Communism used to say that in the future society there would be no more egotists; people would share everything with one another and do everything together. The fundamental principle, "From each according to his abilities, to each according to his needs!", was thought to mean that you would work only as much as you wanted and that everyone could also consume as much as he wanted. First, a basic income for all is introduced, and, then, money was to be abolished. In his day, Party Leader Nikita

Khrushchev promised that the present generation of Soviet people would live in Communism. In the new high-rise apartment complexes, only small kitchens were provided—deliberately, since in the future no one would need a private kitchen. If so, then just to boil water for tea. In the future, people are supposed to eat in free cafeterias, where the professional cooks can prepare everything better anyway. This carefree future was expected at the end of the twentieth century. We were exhorted to keep tightening our belts for just a little while.

While still in elementary school, we learned that we owed this magnificent socialist present and the subsequent even better Communist future to Communists alone. In our family, among all our relatives and even in our circle of acquaintances, however, there were no Communists at all. I saw a few on the street and imagined, in keeping with our Communist education, that they were altogether special human beings. This notion was confirmed when I visited the Museum of the Revolution in Moscow sometime when I was still of elementary-school age. The female museum guide told us that Communists are genuine heroes. We no longer need to invent gods for ourselves; we divinize the proletarians next door. They work day and night; during the Revolution, they gave their lives for poor people; during the war, they could get by for a long time without food and drink and yet still remain righteous and even self-sacrificing. The museum tour made such an impression on me that I ventured to ask carefully a very human question. "Do Communists ever go to the bathroom, too?" The surprised museum guide first took a deep breath and then said, "Yes, they have to go, too, but not as often."

The Remnants

Again and again, lecturers from the Society for Political Education came to our school. Compared with some, Vladimir Ivanovich could tell a good story and portray our fabulous future vividly. "We still must attain Communism, but we have already built socialism", he declared, and then continued: "In every age, people have dreamed of living in a socialist society. We have the good fortune of experiencing socialism, and we describe it as really existing socialism. For now everyone in the world can see that our system is not a fantasy but really exists", the lecturer announced. Every time, he tried once again to convince us about this system. For in socialism, the state provides not only equal rights but also just distribution. It plans everything, thinks everything through, and gives meaning to society. It directs everything to the well-being of the people. We learned that we have available to us the best housing laws, the best medical facilities, the best public transportation, the best productivity, and many other best things in the world. "The only thing that still bothers us", Vladimir Ivanovich said, "is the remnant of the old man that is still hidden in many of us." For me, it was not easy at first to recognize this "remnant", but then I began to look more attentively and could find a whole lot of it all around me.

Public transportation was very convenient in our city. It cost five kopeks to ride the subway or the bus, and only three to ride the streetcar. At first, on every bus in our city there was a conductress who sold tickets and maintained order. Then this was replaced by ticket automats. This automat was basically only a metal box with a roll of tickets. The fare was fixed, but you could put any amount of money into the box and tear off any number of tickets from the roll. "The best control is the passenger's conscience." Everything was good in our public transportation system, except that the buses, which were the only form of public transportation in our city, did not run according to a schedule. They rarely came; they were always full and often very dirty. All that certainly came about because of this "remnant". On the trains, too, there were plenty of "remnants": The trains arrived with delays, the toilets were scarcely cleaned, and the bed linens in the sleeping cars were often poorly dried and sometimes even wet. The train and airplane tickets were satisfactory in themselves, but it was an odyssey to get one during the holidays. Only in the Moscow subway could I find no "remnants". It functioned unobjectionably, was beautiful, clean, and safe. The long-desired future was supposed to look like that.

We could be proud of our healthcare system. We did not need health insurance. You could simply go to a doctor and be treated without cost. You did not have to pay for hospitals, operating rooms, or dentists, either. If you had a fever, there was no need at all to go first to a polyclinic; a phone call and the doctor came to your home the same day. I knew many doctors who worked selflessly and could be reached day and night by the populace. But in medical care, too you could find these "remnants". For example, it was not always user-friendly. Long wait times in the narrow corridors of the polyclinic, bureaucracy, and thoughtlessness were part of it. A Soviet satirical cartoon described the insensitivity of the medical system with two signs on the door of a hospital: "Patients admitted from 10:00 A.M. to 12:00 noon. Corpses discharged from 3:00 to 4:00 P.M."

Socialism did have many advantages, though. In those days, it was not necessary at all to set limits on rent. Apartments were given to citizens for free as needed and according to the number of family members. The monthly fee, including the combined cost of heating and water, was low, and electricity did not cost much, either. The apartments provided by the state could be kept for a lifetime, inherited, and exchanged at will. In reality, though, the battle for an apartment had become a lifelong task for many people. A female colleague of my mother once said with great determination: "If I do not manage to get an apartment from the state in the next ten years, my life will have been in vain." In this department, too, I managed to find many examples of the "remnants" at work. Among my acquaintances, many families with two or three children lived in a 334-square-foot one-room apartment. The six-member family of one of my school friends lived in a farmhouse that consisted of one room that measured only 388 square feet. The farmhouses had no toilets and no running water. There were also so-called communal residences made up of four to six rooms, with one family lodging in each room. In this way, people both in the provinces and in Moscow had somewhat similar goals. The great stated goal—to build up Communism—and the personal goal in life—to get your own apartment from the state.

As time went on, I found so many examples of how the remnants of non-Soviet people disturbed our well-being that I had my doubts about this whole construct. For we could not only hear in lectures about the reality of really existing socialism and the planned economy but also tell jokes like this: Two gardeners are working along a street. One digs holes, and the other immediately fills them in again. When asked what they are doing, they answer: "We are supposed to plant trees. The third guy was supposed to put the saplings into the ground, but he did not come to work today."

Forbidden Bags

My history teacher in senior year was a staunch Communist woman. Once before history class she gave an ardent speech about plastic bags. In her opinion, plastic bags should be forbidden because they are detrimental to the morality of Soviet youth and thus would endanger our very future.

Actually, in those days there were no plastic bags in the Soviet Union. In order to buy groceries, most people used simple shopping nets ("Granny-nets") or fabric bags that they had sewn for themselves. A plastic bag from the West was a jaw-dropping spectacle. To own one was almost like having a pair of Levi's jeans. A couple of enterprising people from my neighborhood even opened a little studio in which they produced plastic bags using a conventional sewing machine. They carefully sewed such bags out of a roll of transparent plastic wrap and fastened pictures from the illustrated papers between the layers of wrap. For a homemade plastic bag, you had to pay two rubles, whereas a hot meal in the school cafeteria cost only twenty kopeks.

Basic needs in the Soviet Union were provided for, yet the people wanted to have more. In those days, food was usually weighed at the counter and wrapped in gray "environmental paper". Very simple one-way plastic bags, which we get today for instance in the produce department, were not free. They were not thrown away but, rather, washed, dried out on the balcony, and used repeatedly. For the people, bright-colored plastic bags and other forms of packaging from the West were proof of a consumer's paradise existing somewhere.

Our history teacher was convinced that carrying plastic bags leads to imitating Western consumerism and, thus, to the moral decay of young people and turns us into selfish consumers according to the capitalist model. Who knows whether this teacher was right? Only a few years later, you could buy such bags everywhere in our country, and, as a result, the Soviet Union, which the whole world feared, collapsed. Even though my teacher then did not care at all about protecting the environment, she would rejoice today about current political decisions in the West. For her ideological opponents—the capitalists—have given up and finally understood that plastic bags can be quite dangerous for the morality of civilization.

Soviet Specialties

The world's freedom is in danger. The U.S. president is an actor, and not much is to be expected politically from Western Europe, for instance, Great Britain, Italy, Austria, or France. Therefore, we must take responsibility for the world's future, for only in our country can every human being really be free. These views were communicated to us in the Soviet Union via the media and political education in the mid-1980s. The majority of the working population even believed, despite all the problems, that freedom, justice, and equal rights were exclusively Soviet specialties, and there was also plenty of evidence for it.

People felt genuinely free to talk about everything and to critique social defects like cowardice, rudeness, alcoholism, or the poor quality of workmanship. Only the topics detrimental to socialism were taboo. Anyone who had not grasped this was considered irresponsible and was compelled to distance himself publicly from his statements and to apologize. The real exchange of political opinions took place, not in public, but in the little kitchens in the high-rise apartment buildings. In our home, we rarely talked about politics, but while visiting our acquaintances, I noticed the politically incorrect kitchen conversations. We children grew up in this system and at first accepted it as the existing normalcy. We also were fortunate to help shape *perestroika* at the age of sixteen. Before then, we had imagined democracy, freedom, and equal rights quite differently.

"Today we have the opportunity to nominate someone for a big prize and to send that person to the Pioneer Camp Artek in the Crimea. Let us decide together who should get this award", our Senior Pioneer Leader said. She opened her documentation, according to which we could quite freely select someone with the following qualifications: a girl from a working family, thirteen years old, and originally from one of the People's Republics. It was an easy task for us, for there was only one girl who qualified. She was unanimously elected.

Equal rights were guaranteed not only for us students but for all Soviet citizens by various quotas. When admitting students to a school or university or giving out places in tour groups, awards, and contest prizes, political offices as well as leadership positions in businesses, the first thing considered was not achievements but, rather, social background and sex. There were quotas for workers, for farmers, for women, and for various nationalities. The quota principle applied also for election to the Supreme Council. Thus all citizens had the opportunity to participate freely in the elections and to toss previously filled-in ballots into the ballot box. It was not customary and not necessary, either, to go into a voting booth—on the ballot there was always only a quota candidate anyway, who certainly could not be crossed off. That was supposed to make participating in elections even less complicated for simple people. Moreover, you could celebrate every election day with concerts and food and drink like a real holiday. The women wore fine clothes, and the men put on their best suits. The voting places opened already at six o'clock in the morning with music from the street loudspeakers. In the cafeterias that were set up specially in the voting places, you could buy delicacies that were otherwise rare. For the schoolchildren such an election became an experience. We looked and dreamed: "When we are grown up, we too will be allowed to cast our ballot." I liked to participate in the accompanying cultural performances.

Once I watched, deeply impressed, as an old veteran decorated with many medals came out of the voting place and walked past me. He patted me on the shoulder and said, "Be proud, my boy, that you were born in our Soviet country. Here everything belongs to the simple people, and you cannot find such a free country anywhere in the world." Even if the man meant it seriously, I doubt today whether "political correctness", quota politics, and ideologies were ever exclusively Soviet specialties.

Liberating Truth

One day a school friend invited me to accompany him around midnight to the Broad Valley. That is the name of a picturesque valley between the Ural Mountains outside the city. At the time, I did not know that this action would become for me not only a test of courage but also a test of honesty. As a matter of course, many people praised the Communist Party at official events and criticized it at home, and for us children that was not a contradiction. We grew up that way and learned to look at this duplicity as a natural rule of behavior. In puberty, one begins to perceive the world differently and to question the existing rules. I, too, had learned with the passage of time to recognize more differences between good and evil. At home, we were always very honest with each other. "Christ is the Truth, and this Truth sets you free", people often said in our house. At school, however, again and again there were situations in which I sensed conflicts of conscience. After the nighttime excursion with my school friend, I was able to experience the liberating power of truth immediately.

The Feast of the Baptism of the Lord plays a special role for Orthodox Christians. It was not on the calendar, but many people knew that this feast is always celebrated on January 19 [on the Julian calendar = January 6 on the Gregorian calendar]. I have already mentioned that in our city there was not one single church. There was a great need, though, to come into contact with the sacred. According to secret informants, the water in natural sources becomes holy water once a year. This happens on the night of Jesus' Baptism. My school friend told me that many people go to the Broad Valley on that night to bring holy water from the mountain spring. I was convinced that at the age of fifteen I was grown up enough to experience this for myself, and I convinced my mother to let me go with this friend.

It was the first time that I went outside the city without being accompanied by adults. On the Feast of the Baptism of the Lord, it was always very cold. The expression "Baptism-chill" is a widely known expression in Russia. That year, the night before the feast was cold but bearable—the temperature was around -4° Fahrenheit. We had dressed warmly and set out at 11:00 P.M. When the illuminated streets were behind us, we began to have an increasingly powerful sense of our adventure. The snow crunched under our feet; the sky was sprinkled with stars. In freezing weather, it would have made no sense to bring flashlights; we simply relied on the moon, which lit this path into the unknown. In itself, a stroll through the woods at night was not forbidden, but with every step it became clearer to us that we were doing something that in the government's view was undesirable or even forbidden. This genuinely harmless action caused us to feel the adrenaline distinctly. In the dark, we could recognize little groups of people or individual travelers far ahead and far behind us. Therefore, we were not alone on this path after all. After three-quarters of an hour on this adventuresome walk, we finally arrived.

The Broad Valley lay under a thick, sparkling blanket of snow. The stars in the clear, frosty sky were far and near at the same time. In the enchanted stillness, you could hear only the soft crackling of the snow and, we suspected, our excited heartbeat, too. All around a hole in the ice stood numerous shadowy figures, which in the moonlight could not be recognized more exactly. No one tried to look the other person in the face, because everyone wanted to remain unknown. Something incomprehensible could be sensed among us at that moment. Around midnight, someone lit a candle and began in a weak, soft voice to recite a prayer in Old Slavonic. This mixture of familiar and unfamiliar words was comprehensible, not in the head, but only in the heart. After the prayer, those present began to fill the bottles that they had brought along with water from the spring. Someone helped my friend and me to draw water in the glass jar that I had brought specifically for this purpose, and we went home. Only when I removed my gloves did I notice that they were covered with a layer of ice. We all drank the water together at home; it was not only cold, but had a particularly fresh and soft taste.

The next day after classes, our teacher ran into me in the hallway and asked: "Now what did you do with the water?" The students in our school had to clean their classrooms themselves every day. I had already forgotten that the teacher had asked me to throw out the dirty water from the bucket standing in our classroom. That day I had classroom service and consequently had to change the water in the cleaning bucket. Because of my nocturnal adventure, I was not only tired and sleepy but also still mentally preoccupied with the event in the Broad Valley.

"How does our teacher know that I was at the spring of water yesterday? How will I be punished, and what excuse can I give?" Several scenes played out in my head at that moment. "The water was not for me, but for my grandmother", I answered spontaneously.

The teacher surely could not understand what the water

from the cleaning bucket had to do with my grandmother, and she carefully asked, "Are you all right?" At that moment, I became aware that out of anxiety I had lied and shifted the responsibility to my grandmother. Not long before that, we had spoken about manliness during a classroom discussion. To be manly was to speak the truth always. I did not ask myself then whether there was a difference between manly and womanly truth, but in any case I wanted to react in a manly way. But I had reacted to my teacher dishonestly and felt my face turning red. Interiorly, I asked God for His help and decided to confess the truth, despite all the dangers. "Excuse me. Honestly, it was my idea, and I brought the water not only for my grandmother but for all of us." In my teacher's expression I could read not only confusion but the need for further clarification. "Don't worry. I brought the water home for the first time; I never did that until now. And nothing is left of it, either; we already drank it all", I added, ready at that moment to suffer all the consequences as a real man. Instead, I heard her desperate words, "I think that you had better go home and rest. We will clean the classroom today without your participation." She walked away, and then I realized that we had spoken the whole time at cross purposes.

The Feast of the Baptism of the Lord brought me not only new spiritual experiences but also a pleasant confirmation of the fact that the truth sets you free, sometimes even from a classroom duty.

The Coveted Vitamin B

In school, we learned that every kind of work and every occupation is honorable. There was one occupation, though,
that was especially highly regarded. That was being a store
clerk. Everyone wanted to establish contacts and develop
relations with store clerks; at every party, they were desir-
able guests. In our system of distributions and regulations,
salesmen were in the best position and, despite all the con-
trols, could help determine the distribution of groceries and
goods. What you did not find in the grocery store you could
get via the side entrance. Even those who monitored the
people not infrequently made their purchases in this way.
Those who knew a store clerk, or, even better, the store
manager, had an advantage in any case.

Since our family was not from the city, we were completely excluded from Vitamin B. My mother had to wait
for hours in line in order to purchase certain groceries. In
line you exchanged news stories, met new people, and some
people even started their family while standing in line. Sometimes, though, all the trouble was in vain, because it could
happen that the goods for which you were waiting ran out
just before you reached the counter. Purchasing foods like
meat, sausage, or butter was always an adventure. It was possible for our situation to improve for a short time, though,
when I became acquainted with a girl.

Once my mother brought meat and butter home with

her and told a story about a surprising encounter. When she tried to buy only a trifle, the clerk asked her for a considerably larger sum of money. Before my mother could ask anything, she received a piece of meat wrapped in paper and also a stick of butter. It was not at all necessary to ask whether someone would like to buy meat or butter. Everyone wanted to have that. My mother could not understand at all how she deserved this good fortune. "I am Nina Ivanovna," the clerk said, "and I know your son . . ."

My school friend Oleg and I were in eighth grade when we became friends with Elena from the tenth grade. We visited her several times at her house, and each time were very glad about the delicious food, but did not know that her funny, talkative mother was a store clerk. Later, I stopped often to see Nina Ivanovna at her general store, for she liked to chat with me. Once she even asked me to help her. I went in through the side entrance and was surprised that you could find everything in the storeroom. Quite naïvely, I thought that probably Nina Ivanovna had not yet managed to bring these groceries to the counter, and being a helpful person, I put them on a cart and brought them into the salesroom. Rarely have I been in the middle of such joyful customers. And yet I noticed that something was not right, because Nina Ivanovna was not particularly happy about my help. Her daughter Elena told me a few days later that my help was no longer needed in the store. The only advantageous connection our family ever had started up and stopped again so unexpectedly. What we learned in school was true, therefore: naturally occurring vitamins make people strong and healthy, but artificial ones have only a limited effect and often are not absorbed. This is particularly evident in the case of Vitamin B.

Dangerous Courage

There were many good things in my childhood and youth. There were many good things, and there were meetings. Meetings of the Young Pioneers and *Komsomoltsi* [members of the Communist Youth League], meetings of various committees and panels, and also the usual class meetings. No one dared to ask whether these meetings had any significance at all, because they served an important pedagogical purpose. They were supposed to make a collective out of us students or, as we say today, a team; they were supposed to teach us to discuss all problems together and in this way to learn socialist democracy. For me, such a class meeting became in fact an initiation into Soviet collectivism.

At the end of eighth grade, we were between fourteen and fifteen years old. On account of his discipline problems, Kostya had had to repeat a grade and, therefore, was older than we were. He did not manage to subordinate himself to our school system; he was insolent to grown-ups and rebelled in any way he could. His many pranks gave him an air of authority in the estimation of many other "bad boys". He and I were not exactly friends, but there was some mutual respect between us. Several times I visited him at home and felt that he was an intelligent, well-read, inquisitive person who made an odd impression in our surroundings. Now he became the topic of our class meeting. The collective was supposed to show him its deep dislike, isolate him, and in this way take care of class discipline.

After our teacher and several activists had condemned Kostya in strong terms, I spoke up and said that he had many good qualities and could be a good friend. From that moment on, not Kostya, but I was suddenly at the center of the event. Our class spokesperson said that people like me were socially immature. You have to look at yourself critically first, and only then can you venture to make statements like mine. Suddenly all my conscious and unconscious sins were held up to the light of the assembly. I did not do my homework regularly; I gave it to others to be copied; and although I was always present, I lived my own life. All at once the pieces of the puzzle fit together and proved what a socially unbearable human being I was. I was called to the front and had to stand before the whole class and look my classmates in the eye. Not one positive word could be heard about me that evening. When it got late, we went home with different feelings. Our teacher was content that some students had shown a mature, socialistic attitude toward life. Our class spokesperson was proud that she was able to stand up for order in the class and, thus, for the good of society. Most of the students were glad that the meeting was over and that no one had addressed them in it. Outside it was dark and dank; I remained standing alone on the street and did not feel like going anywhere. For the first time in my life, I experienced as a teenager what loneliness feels like and did not know how I should cope with it. If everybody is against me, it would be best to disappear forever.

The next day, our class spokesperson told me that I should not be mad at her but grateful. She explained that the previous day she had only done her civic duty and had shown civic courage. She was right, because we were raised that way. Civic duty and civic courage had the highest moral priority in our education. Even as Young Pioneers, we learned the story about Pavlik Morosov, who at the age of thirteen out of civic courage turned his father in to the Soviet authorities and even testified against him in court. Today we may argue about this, but many people who reported their suspicious colleagues, neighbors, and family members and exposed them to political repression did not always do it out of personal interest or with ill will, but often out of inner conviction and for the good of society. An altogether ordinary class meeting taught me how fast it can happen and how it feels to be judged and abandoned by everyone. From such a harmless episode, you could also learn that even civic courage can be dangerous.

Sobering Realization

After eighth grade came a surprising honor. For the first time, there was a school trip to the Golden Ring, and I was allowed to go on it. The Golden Ring is a series of old Russian towns north of Moscow that are among the best-known historical sites in Russia. For me, it was a magnificent opportunity to delve even deeper into history. Many of us had never been so far away from home before and could ride for the first time in a long-distance train. We used this occasion to get to know each other better and even to try our luck at being ladies' men.

When we arrived, we stayed in two large rooms: in the one, we fifteen boys with our gym teacher; and in the other, fifteen girls with one of our school principals. In the evening, when we were already in bed, the teacher told adult jokes, for which we of course already felt mature enough. During the day, we went from museum to museum. The churches had been closed for a long time, but many museums and displays were set up in the buildings. Once, though, we came to a church that was still being used, in which something liturgical was happening right then. Many had never before seen a Divine Liturgy and were rather curious. Since both our escorts were professed Communists, we had little hope of being allowed to go in. We asked very carefully whether we could look in briefly and received a surprising answer: "At the moment we cannot hear your question and at the moment we do not see what you are doing for the next quarter of an hour." All clear. One minute later, we were all in the church. Of course we took pains to overlook the fact that our two escorts were also trying to hide in a corner.

We discovered during the trip that we had an opportunity not only to see the sights but also to look with wide-awake eyes at the girls traveling with us. In our class at that time, there were thirty-one students, twenty-one of them boys. We had been acquainted with our girls for eight years and therefore found them not particularly interesting, whereas the girls from other classes seemed mysterious and attractive. Now I, too, had selected and gawked at a dream candidate. She seemed not only pretty but above all gentle, affectionate, humorous, and well-behaved. Our rapprochement consisted of little signs of attention, now a dandelion, now a nice word or a praline. And it was not all in vain: this was demonstrated by a bar of chocolate that I received from her on the day of our departure.

On the return trip, our boys thought that it was fun, despite my protests, to throw various objects, including chicken bones that had been gnawed clean, out of the train window. In doing so, no one could have imagined that all these objects did not fall down but rather flew into the train again two windows farther back and landed on the berth of my dream girl. Shortly thereafter, I was able to get acquainted with her from an altogether different side. She threw everything that she had collected at my feet and despite my apology and numerous attempts to explain everything, cursed like a truck driver hauling beer. To this day, I do not know which one of us was more disappointed about the other. All at once, I was an idiot in her opinion, and I was able to become acquainted with her from a completely different perspective. All at once, nothing was left of the gentle, affectionate, humorous object of my romantic fantasies. The girls in our class were no worse than the others after all. So the trip helped me very simply to realize that the cherries in the neighbor's garden do not always taste sweeter.

Opium for the People

Since the Soviet flag was still too heavy for me at that time, usually I would have had to carry balloons like the other elementary-school children. "We entrust to you our General Secretary", someone wearing a red armband told me. I got the portrait of the Party Chief Leonid Brezhnev fastened to a pole. So for the first time in my life I participated in a demonstration. Twice a year, on Workers' Day and on October Revolution Day, festive demonstrations took place everywhere in the Soviet Union. In Moscow and in some major cities, there were also military parades on October Revolution Day. Only once in my life have I experienced one live. But in our city, too, the demonstrations were festive. Optimistic marches from the street loudspeakers created the appropriate mood. Every school, every business took part in the demonstrations and followed a truck festively decorated for the purpose. I did not like marching with the children and managed to get off from the school group each time so as to go with my mother's business. For many years in a row I got to carry the General Secretary. "You got a heavy burden; just look at how much metal you have to lug around", my fellow marchers laughed, pointing at the countless decorations and medals that were depicted on the jacket of Brezhnev's uniform. When we walked past the main square, we had to raise our flags, banners, and portraits of Communist dignitaries high. The party officials on the platform that was built on the square called over the loudspeaker slogans like "The Party is the reason, the honor, and the conscience of our era." Those demonstrating answered with a loud "Hurrah!" The procession, including the time it took to get into formation, lasted between two and three hours. Afterward everyone went home to celebrate privately with their families and colleagues.

When I was elementary-school age, I liked to demonstrate with the grown-ups. In terms of how they were organized, you could compare those demonstrations with a Mardi Gras parade, except without the carnival atmosphere, without humor, without costumes, and without camels. Later, though, I began to ask questions that had no answers: For whom are we demonstrating on these days? What are we trying to show? Why do we carry photos of the Politburo members in procession past the platform with the local Party officials, as though they had never seen them before? No one out of my circle of acquaintances, at least, showed any interest in discussing these questions with me: Demonstrations seemed to be just as self-evident as heaven and earth. Fortunately, I was able to turn with these questions to the mother of my school friend Erik: Anfissa Anvarovna. Being a librarian, she was very well-read. She read a book a night on average and always had time to listen to my ideas, to read my naïve poems and initial literary attempts, and also for all my questions. "Just come to our house after the next demonstration and celebrate with us", Anfissa Anvarovna said, after I had expressed once again my doubts about the meaning of demonstrations. I was fifteen years old then.

I was glad that this time I had carried a bunch of balloons instead of a red flag, and after the demonstration we stopped by Erik's house. First, we watched the remainder of the festive parade from his window and then sat down at the table. There were *pelmeni*—meat-filled pockets of dough—and for dessert a torte from the local bread factory. "The meaning of every holiday lies in the fact that we have the opportunity to come together and celebrate", Anfissa Anvarovna said. At that, Erik's father put a glass of vodka on the table and grinned: "Here is the opium for the people." In his day, Karl Marx described religion as the "opium of the people", and Vladimir Lenin changed this saying to "opium for the people". Even though Erik's father had applied this expression to the vodka, suddenly my eyes were opened: Communism had simply become a new religion.

Only later was I able to discover many parallels between the Communist Party and the Church. Marx, Engels, and Lenin were the Holy Trinity; their works were supposed to be studied like Sacred Scripture. The pictures of the Party leaders and members of the government were carried in procession like icons; Party hymns were sung instead of church hymns. First Communion and Confirmation could be compared with acceptance into the Pioneer Organization and into the Communist Youth League. The Revolutionaries were honored like martyrs, and many rituals were established for the populace. In all this, an important role was played by a carefully thought-out symbolism that even children learned to interpret. Hammer and sickle showed the union of workers and farmers; the five-pointed red star—the unity of the proletarians on all five continents; the color red—the blood of the Revolutionaries; the hand raised over the head in the Young Pioneers' salute showed that general interests had priority over private ones. It seemed that this faith helped many people to give meaning and order to their lives. The development of ideologies into secular religions shows, incidentally, that human beings who were created by God cannot live without faith. If one religion is forbidden, another will eventually be created. In the Soviet Union we lived, therefore, in a deeply religious society, in which the government's world view was supposed to become opium for the people.

My First Pay

Many people can remember well how they first earned money. I received my first remuneration as a young journalist at the age of fourteen. The amount was a little more than four rubles. At the time, I found a meeting of the book club so exciting that I definitely wanted to write a report about it. So I wrote my first article and sent it to the district newspaper. When my report was published several days later, many people spoke to me about it. One teacher said that she did not think that I was capable of writing such an article by myself. I accepted the challenge to keep writing and soon became the only *Yunkor*—young correspondent—in the city.

As a budding journalist, I still had no sense of what was appropriate or politically correct for those times and wrote just as I thought. My essays about the senselessness of organized free time at a distant place or about the local disco and breakdancing were the talk of the town. I regret today my critical report about the medical emergency services, in which I in my ignorance described how slow the emergency crew members were. Only years later did I learn that I had offended several people; a female physician told me that my report was still being discussed among her colleagues.

A journalist told me later in a confidential conversation what I should be especially careful of and what the difference was between our media and those in the capitalist world. The capitalist media sell information and do not reflect on their social responsibility. The socialist media, in contrast, pursue the goal not only of informing but most importantly of enlightening. Through their honest presentations, the socialist media should educate people to be good citizens and help them to appreciate the advantages of our political system. After this conversation, I understood also that in the West the Church cares about people's conscience, whereas in the Soviet Union, the Communist Party is responsible for the conscience of the citizens with the help of the media. Since I already felt grown up at that moment, I began to write something that was supposed to help open the eyes of the stupid readers to our ideological advantages. Easier said than done. Everything that I tried to write seemed not only naïve but simply stupid. After several drafts ended up in the wastebasket, I understood that political journalism was not my calling.

After a conversation with another journalist, I was deeply moved by his candor and fascinated by his heretical thoughts: "Read the newspapers, but form your own opinion. We are all human beings and none of us has a patent on the truth."

The true meaning of newspapers was revealed to me by Uncle Kolya—an elderly man who lived on the ground floor of our high-rise apartment complex. He praised above all the newspaper *Pravda*, which was particularly well suited for filleting pickled herrings. The newspaper *Trud*, in his opinion, was good as packing material, table covering, and toilet paper. It does not leave stains and smells less of printer's ink than the others. He did not say for what purposes he used the newspapers with my contributions.

April Fools!

At the age of fifteen, all boys had to have a medical examination. During mine, they discovered a dangerous change in my leg bone. At first they suspected tuberculosis—a terrible prognosis. After being examined at a specialized hospital, I was sent to the best regional clinic. To our joy and relief, we got an "all-clear" signal—no tuberculosis. Nevertheless, I was not allowed to leave the hospital. For several months, various tests were administered, and the doctors looked at me sympathetically, without giving me a diagnosis.

One day, I had the opportunity to look at my medical chart and on it read frightening news—cancer. I spoke with no one about it. At that time, cancer was incurable; it was not a diagnosis, but a death sentence. In the whole world, there was only one person who could help me in this situation. He was invisible—and yet He was there. In my childlike trust, I had no doubt that God knows exactly what is good for me. The thought did not occur to me to ask Him "Why?" I just began to pray more intensely. I prayed where the others could not see me—during my walks through long corridors of the hospital and also under the blankets. If Jesus wants to, He can certainly see to it that nothing is left of this cancer. I spoke with Him like a small, naïve boy and promised Him to promote love in my surroundings. I had no idea how quickly I would have an opportunity to do so.

After four months, a panel of doctors decided on surgery.

I lay in a room with five beds together with four grown-
ups, all of them seriously ill. Beside my bed was the bed
of a young man named Vlad who had fallen in love with
the nurse Larissa. He constantly spoke about it but did not
have the courage to talk to her. No one knew how we could
help this guy Vlad. On the day of the operation, I looked
at them all dramatically: Who knows whether I would see
them all again? I prayed for Vlad, too, and assured him that
we would all have a fine future.

On the day after my operation, I was still confined to
bed with a high fever. When I opened my eyes early in the
morning, I wondered what day it was. It was April 1. Playing an April Fool's joke on someone would have lightened
the mood in the room. But they were all still sleeping. Now
Nurse Larissa looked through the door. Young people like
me often act spontaneously, without reflecting on the consequences. So I called out, in a voice still weak after surgery:
"Nurse, nurse, my roommate is not doing well." The nurse
went to Vlad's bed and asked very carefully, "Hey, how are
you doing?" Vlad was still fast asleep and did not react to
these words. The nurse was concerned; she sat down on
the edge of his bed, took his hand and asked him again:
"How are you?" There was no answer except for a deep
exhalation. The situation became more and more serious.
All the other roommates were already awake and observed
the rescue operation. Now the poor nurse urgently had to
rouse the unconscious man. She remained quite calm and
professional and began to slap him on both cheeks. When
Vlad opened his eyes, he could not understand what was
happening. Beside him on the bed sat his dream woman,
who was looking at him and asking, "Are you unwell?"
Vlad's grin spread over his whole face, and he murmured.
"Oh, I'm doing really, really well!" I congratulated them all

with an "April Fools!", and the whole room was filled with loud laughter.

I had to stay in bed for another six weeks. They drilled through the bone and kept it elevated with counterweights. My first two steps around the bed caused tears of joy. In late May, I was discharged from the hospital. The surgeon spoke quite frankly with me this time: "We made such a big incision because we were looking for cancer. Your bone was not entirely healthy, but we found no cancer." He recommended that during my recuperation I should eat a lot of protein, which was not easy at all, given the food shortages then. My Aunt Maria managed somehow to purchase for me a large, over two-pound can of black caviar. And so, for the only time in my life, I could chow down caviar and had to. I started learning again to walk and knew that God can turn everything to the good. The pains and the fears are long since forgotten, but April 1 became one of my favorite days of the year. It is worthwhile to give someone else a little joy, even when you yourself are not doing so well.

The Victory of Tautology

One October evening, all the students in the senior class were invited to a meeting. "Comrades!", the woman secretary of the Communist Youth League addressed our school. "We are mature enough to think not only about our matriculation exams but also about the most important test of our life. We can prove this right away by our participation in the 'Lenin Certificate' program!" At the end of the meeting, each of us received a preprinted notebook the size of a postcard. From that moment on, we were automatically enrolled in a voluntary program of spiritual growth for Soviet youth.

The Lenin Certificate was supposed to attest that we were reading works by Vladimir Lenin in our free time and thus pursuing our Communist self-development. First, each one of us had to formulate goals for personal growth and have these confirmed by schoolmates. These goals were recorded in a separate little notebook and at the end of every quarter were evaluated independently after an examination of conscience. These goals included, for example, improving academic achievements, correcting character traits, service for the common good, and eliminating bad habits. It was expected that at the end of the school year everyone would have his comrades testify to his personal development in a class meeting on this topic.

No wonder only a few students were enthusiastic about

the Lenin Certificate. Only a few, but some, nevertheless. In every place, there will be activists who want to make plans not only for themselves but, above all, for others. One of them had already confided to me his existential wisdom: "When you supervise others, no one will dare to supervise you." For those who did not see themselves as overseers of others but also did not want to be supervised, only one option was left: not to take the activists seriously.

My good friend Oleg offered to fill out our little notebooks together. What goals should we write down in it? As Young Pioneers, we had already worked on campaigns of nature conservation and friendship among peoples. In preparation for studies at the teachers' university, I was attending then a course for future teachers and was very active in youth work. That would be only one point, though, and you needed at least five. We looked for a way to avoid lying and yet to get through this campaign without problems.

After joint deliberation, we managed to draft a program for our self-development, and each of us had the other confirm it. On one page were listed works by Lenin that were in the school curriculum anyway. On the page with personal resolutions, we wrote the following five points:

1. To fill out the little notebook provided for the certificate.
2. To reflect on Point 1 in light of Leninism.
3. To check regularly my work on Points 1 and 2.
4. Continually to improve on my performance of Points 1 through 3.
5. To inform my comrade about possible difficulties with Points 1 through 4.

Satisfied with our resolutions, we set these notebooks aside, and the school year went on. Until April of the following year, there seemed to be no more talk about the

Lenin Certificate. Then we had to deal again with our resolutions from last year. Oleg and I marked all five points
as accomplished and submitted our notebooks to be graded.
At the class meeting for the conclusion of the Lenin Certificate, however, we both had a rather queasy feeling. Some
notebooks were to be selected by chance from the stack and
evaluated in front of the whole class. What would we say
and what would we have to listen to if ours were picked?
The other students had likewise set goals that were easy—
but not as insolent—and were praised for their good work.
The weaknesses of some were pointed out, and they got
some time for remedial work. We two were not mentioned
at all.

"It is over!" we thought, and we went home relieved. The
following day, the school administrator in charge of educational work called us to her office. Our two notebooks lay
on her desk. Oleg and I looked at each other for a moment
and prepared ourselves interiorly for the worst. "Yesterday
we forgot to speak about your Lenin Certificate", the administrator said and unexpectedly pinned on the chest of
each of us a red badge depicting Lenin's head. "You pro-
posed five points, and you achieved all five. We are proud
of you! You are behaving like genuine Soviet men!"

In the mid-1980s, only a few people were interested in
Communist self-development; the speeches and addresses
became more and more meaningless and tautological. That
is exactly how it was with our Lenin Certificate, too. Neither of us had read our notebook; all that counted were
the formal results. From this perspective, we had to say that
the school administrator was right: We in fact behaved like
most Soviet men: just like altogether normal children of our
times.

For Whom the Ballet Dances

"Our great advantage is political stability", our female and male citizens used to say. As long as I could remember, we always had the same Party Leader and Head of State. He scarcely decided anything, he gave speeches that were ideological rather than pragmatic, and he seemed to everyone to be irreplaceable. There were many jokes and anecdotes about Leonid Brezhnev, and yet he was beloved and had the general support of the people. Life seemed stable, and no one worried about his own future, much less about the future of the country.

The death of the old, sick Brezhnev came, nevertheless, as a surprise to many people. They had the feeling that he would be the head of the country forever. The next day, his portrait stood at the school entrance, decorated with black bunting and flowers. I was thirteen years old at the time. Some students said that Brezhnev's time was up anyway. Our physics teacher intervened in the discussion and appealed to our conscience. He said that we had just lost a decisive peacemaker and that, because of it, the situation in the world was becoming more and more serious.

Three days of national mourning began. Much to our satisfaction, the day of the burial was declared a school holiday. All entertainment programs on television were replaced on those days by classical music and ballet. For us, it was a unique situation, in which an all-encompassing mood of sadness and depression prevailed. This unique situation was repeated fifteen months later when the next head of state, Yuri Andropov, died. And after another thirteen months, the same situation due to the death of the next paramount leader, Konstantin Chernenko. On each of these occasions, ballet was shown on television, above all *Swan Lake*. Maybe it was because of the scene with the dying swan or something about the history of this music. Pyotr Tchaikovsky finished this composition in Easter week, during which Orthodoxy traditionally commemorates the dead.

With the election of the relatively young Gorbachev, the series of major state funerals was over, but the perception of ballet was entrenched for many more years. "They definitely killed him", the lady next door called from her window to another neighbor. She had turned on the television, seen *Swan Lake*, and drawn from it only one conclusion: that now Gorbachev, too, was dead. By then people probably no longer knew whether the death of a politician caused a ballet broadcast or vice versa. *Swan Lake* was broadcast for the last time in a political context during the August Coup in 1991. The whole country was kept in ignorance about the imprisoned Mikhail Gorbachev, while on television this ballet could be seen again. Four months later, the Soviet Union collapsed.

"For Whom the Ballet Dances"—that is how the question in the title of Ernest Hemingway's famous novel, *For Whom the Bell Tolls*, would be formulated in this context. *Swan Lake* is indisputably one of the best-known works of music in the world. In connection with a TV broadcast, it also is reminiscent of the stagnation and decline of an empire. For many people, it was a warning; for others a sign of a turning point. In other words, a ballet for the future.

The Diploma

It started with a solemn assembly in the gymnasium. All the teachers and parents were there. We celebrated the last school bell. A girl from the first grade had the honor of ringing a little golden bell and announcing the last school class of our life. Everything about that day was different. The teachers did not seem so strict now. The school administrators did not talk about abstract Communist goals but suddenly addressed us in an altogether humane way: "Soon you will no longer be students. We have done everything possible to prepare you for life in the big world, now it is up to you yourselves." Farewells in Russia are always sentimental. One female teacher began to cry. Tears could be seen in the eyes of many parents, too, and even of some of us. Everyone sensed that the grown-ups meant their words and feelings seriously. By the end of school, we had finally learned to get along with each other in class. Now we were trying to understand the fact that we were no longer children. To be exact, we were between sixteen and seventeen years old.

In my day, only ten years of school were needed for a diploma. You were admitted to first grade only after your sixth birthday. Elementary school lasted for three years. After eighth grade, it was possible to go to a vocational school or to a more academic secondary school. After tenth grade, you received a diploma. At that time, there were no *Gym-*

nasien [German college preparatory schools]; all the schools throughout the country followed the same system. School instruction concluded at the end of May with the last school bell. After that, there were final examinations in literature, mathematics, history, biology, physics, chemistry, and foreign languages. Right after the last exam, the big graduation dance took place.

On graduation day, we ourselves did not know whether we were still children or already grown up. Girls had festive clothes made for them to wear at the graduation dance, and the boys bought themselves suits and ties. Afterward, there was a little graduation tour in rented buses through the locality and a festive dinner in the school cafeteria. The parents themselves cooked. "Thank God!" we thought, because it took special training to cook as badly as the cafeteria cooks did. Our parents performed their task well. Right at that time, the government had started a major public service campaign against alcoholism, so at our prom there was neither beer nor wine. Instead, there was live music by a genuine band. After the exams, the teachers had become even friendlier and more humane. The teacher of our class and two female administrators took my good friend Paul, me, and two girls with them to the faculty lounge to drink some champagne with us there secretly. Until then, we had concealed from the teachers everything that was not allowed; now our teachers concealed together with us the forbidden champagne from our government that cares about everything. At four in the morning, we all went outside together to greet the first sunrise of our adult life. When we noticed that some teachers were already gone, we went to their houses and loudly sang the school songs under their windows. No one in the neighborhood was mad at us—everyone knew that on this day, in all the schools in the country, a sentimental farewell from school was celebrated and, at the same time, the beginning of adult life.

For such a long time I had wished finally to be a grown-up. One week after the graduation dance, I would turn seventeen. I would then apply to the university and begin my own life. But that night we all enjoyed our last opportunity to be schoolchildren. The graduation dance went without odd incidents or surprises. Everything was in order. We lived in a great and, from our perspective then, secure country that promised a happy future. Hopefully, sentimentally, happily, and confidently, we looked forward to the future. The school had given us official diplomas, "certificates of maturity" [*Reifezeugnisse*]. Now life was to confirm for each one of us whether we actually would be mature and when.

Epilogue

School was closed, the graduation dance had been celebrated, we had our diplomas in hand. We had learned something, talked a lot, and reflected a lot about our future. And yet not only we but also our teachers and educators, our parents and everyone who made an impression on our lives had no idea what awaited us.

On June 23, 1986, when we went our separate ways after the graduation dance, we did not know that our class would never meet again with full attendance. At seventeen years of age, we were children who already felt like grown-ups. We were ready to make independent decisions and to take responsibility for our lives. But we could not have imagined that some of us would do military service in Afghanistan one year later and, instead of a dummy rifle, would have to carry genuine machine guns and become acquainted with death. It was a surprise to us that one of our fellow students brought a child into the world shortly after the graduation dance and started a family. It was unimaginable that the most secure State of workers and farmers, founded for eternity, would collapse only five years after we completed school.

In this book, I have tried to tell about the fate of millions of human beings with little stories from my childhood. Surely everyone had his own circumstances and collected his own experiences. And yet we were alike, because we were supposed to grow up into correct Soviet men and women according to the same pattern. Through revolutions and repressions, Soviet citizens tried to build up the most just society of all times and also an earthly paradise. This paradise was supposed to do without God and to divinize man. Millions of enthusiasts went along with this experiment and did not or could not admit to themselves that the results did not square with the original dream.

Even today, all over the world, there are people who find socialist ideas, Communism, or other authoritarian or totalitarian world views attractive and would like certain ideological concepts to be adopted. Today there are also many attempts to free our planet not only from religion and Church but also from God. With childish naïveté many people follow these ideas.

An old Russian historian Vasily Klyuchevsky compared history with a light: the light from the past that illuminates the future. May the encounters with Communists, atheists, and also nice people that are related in this book help us to become grown up, to learn to appreciate freedom and democracy, and to give God more room in our lives.

Outline

What an unusual look at a bygone world: Alexander N. Krylov's memoirs, recorded in episodic fragments, of his childhood and adolescent years in the Soviet Union provide surprising, informative, amusing, sad, consoling, and exciting reading for readers to whom the ruined colossal Communist empire is and was literally *terra incognita*—unknown territory. It is a retrospect on a young life of many privations, narrated with gentle irony but without any bitterness.

And what an unusual author: Alexander Krylov, born 1969, grew up in a German-Russian family, lost his father at an early age, experienced atheism as the state religion but also had a grandmother and a mother who kept their Catholic faith. After his school years he had a meteoric academic career. By age thirty, Krylov was already assistant dean of the Faculty for Business and Management at his university in Moscow. In the year 2000, he came to Germany and worked as an instructor and later a professor in Bremen and Berlin. He wrote numerous academic publications.

The incisive turning point in Krylov's life, however, was yet to come. "On Easter Monday, 2011, I woke up and knew that the day had arrived", he relates. For more than nine years, he had already sensed a vocation to become a Catholic priest, but now the decision was made. After studying theology, he was ordained first a deacon and then, on June 3, 2016, a Catholic priest by Cardinal Woelki of Cologne. In

Professor Dr. Alexander Krylov the Archdiocese of Cologne now has a priest with an extraordinarily exciting biography. About the present volume he says: "I have lent myself out personally so as to tell what life is like in an authoritarian system." He has done this successfully in an extremely entertaining way.

—*Klaus Nachbaur*